diagnostic and criterion-referenced reading tests:

review and evaluation

Edited by
Leo M. Schell
Kansas State University

for the IRA evaluation of tests committee

INTERNATIONAL READING ASSOCIATION
800 Barksdale Road   Newark, Delaware 19711

*LB
1050.46
D5*

INTERNATIONAL READING ASSOCIATION

Copyright 1981 by the
International Reading Association, Inc.
Library of Congress Cataloging in Publication Data
Main entry under title:
Diagnostic and criterion referenced reading tests.

  Bibliography: p.
  1. Reading—Ability testing.   2. Criterion
referenced tests.   I. Schell, Leo M.   II.
International Reading Association.
Evaluation of Tests Committee.
LB1050.46.D5   428.4'076   81-11820
ISBN 0-87207-731-4   AACR2

ii

Contents

Foreword

The field of assessment in reading is currently in a state of vigorous activity and change. New tests are being developed and older tests are being revised and updated; in fact, the testing process itself is under heavy scrutiny. Reading specialists need to be not only knowledgeable about testing in general, but aware of current developments. To study each available reading test in detail is a very time consuming job, requiring a fair amount of sophistication in both measurement and curriculum. This book will facilitate the process considerably.

The old categorizations of reading tests are fading rapidly. The assumption that a diagnostic reading test must be administered individually no longer holds; it isn't even clear where we would draw the line between a survey test and an instructional or diagnostic test. Proponents of criterion referenced tests tried hard to create a dichotomy with the so-called norm referenced tests, but we now have criterion referenced tests with norms and criterion referenced interpretations of norm referenced tests. A closer look will reveal that the two types of test have, indeed, become so similar that the dichotomy makes less sense than ever. In the process, the developers of the two types of test influenced each other, a phenomenon which deserves closer scrutiny.

The most persistent and complex problem for those of us who develop reading tests is still the issue, *What are the reading skills?* One is often led to believe that the more test subscores we can get for a student, the more diagnostic the test. And the development of "reading management systems" has often supported this contention. But are the "skills" which we are diagnosing really distinct skills? Can differential measurement be supported by empirical data? Often it cannot. This is particularly true for the "comprehension skills." This publication points out that we do have one good criterion for making such a judgment—the test manual's table of intercorrelations.

We have gone through a period of management by objectives, with the lists of objectives becoming longer and longer, every objective having a criterion referenced test. The entire system forced many schools to teach children to read by the "minutia method." But the reading test results kept telling us that these sub-subskills were really not separate entities, that they were highly intercorrelated, representing more general skills. Children do learn to generalize both with respect to decoding skills and reading comprehension, and instruction doesn't need to be differentiated down to each individual phoneme-grapheme relationship which the student may have failed on a specific item. Individual items or even groups of two or three items do not have that kind of diagnostic power. But the more important issue is: At what level of specificity do we need to teach? Assessment would have to be guided by that principle.

Reading tests can be used, then, to determine the level of specificity at which instruction might take place. We have often seen survey tests criticized for testing young children on words that do not appear in their basal readers, the assumption being that it makes a difference. But the test results tell us that if the test words are no more complex, conceptually and phonetically, than the words taught, it doesn't make any difference. That's how children acquire the reading process. In fact, one could argue as cogently that reading tests *should* contain some words which have not been taught, to determine the extent to which each student has learned to generalize the reading skills which have been acquired.

Reading tests do not exist in isolation, they must relate back to the curriculum and instructional objectives. But the point has been made that these objectives must have an empirical base and that tests can be helpful in establishing such a base. Tests can be used, then, not only to study pupil achievement but also to give us insights into how the reading process is acquired. This places great demands on the tests used, and test selection becomes more critical than ever. A book such as this one, therefore, should be particularly timely.

Bjorn Karlsen
Sonoma State University

This Book: Why and How

Leo M. Schell
Kansas State University

The test reviews in this book are intended to help concerned educators to select the best available diagnostic and criterion-referenced reading tests for their purposes—and to shun those which are questionable, inappropriate, or unsatisfactory.

Each year the reading skills of thousands of children are evaluated by diagnostic and/or criterion-referenced reading tests, and decisions about the reading strengths and needs of these children are based upon these results. But test results can be only as sound as the test producing them. Quality tests yield sound data; questionable tests, questionable data. Regrettably, quality tests may be scarcer than we suspect.

Oscar Buros (1972) one of the foremost authorities on test evaluation, though not talking specifically about reading tests, claimed that "at least half of the tests currently on the market should never have been published." James Popham (1978) one of the most ardent proponents of criterion-referenced tests, has become so disenchanted with the quality of some of these tests that he recently lamented that some "are less fit for schools than they are for paper shredders." Buros' *Mental Measurements Yearbooks* (1972, 1978) are superb test evaluation resources but are usually found only in college libraries or in offices of curriculum directors in medium and large sized school districts; seldom does a reading or classroom teacher have ready access to these resources. Hence this book.

1

The reviews in this monograph are intended to make readers more knowledgeable, evaluative, cautious, and professional. Consumer advocates have recently begun to demand that canned and packaged foods plainly state what the contents are so that the potential buyer will have more to rely on than misleading names or enticing photos on labels. Educators wanting the best for their students would be well advised to expect and demand precisely the same kind of information from all tests, including those labeled "diagnostic" and "criterion-referenced."

To determine which tests to review, a list of 34 individual and group diagnostic and criterion-referenced tests was compiled by the editor and sent to the nine members of the International Reading Association Evaluation of Tests Committee and to directors of reading in 35 cities of at least 250,000 population in 25 states. They were asked to check 10-15 tests they considered important enough to be reviewed in an IRA monograph and to add any not shown in the IRA list which they believed should have been included. Sixty percent of the surveys were returned. An arbitrary decision was made to include the 12 most frequently listed tests.

Members of the Evaluation of Tests Committee wrote most of the reviews; reading educators nominated by members of the committee wrote the remaining reviews. Each review was critiqued by a reading educator who independently familiarized him/herself with the test before scrutinizing the review. The review was revised as necessary by the original reviewer. Four reviewers selected by IRA independently reviewed the manuscript and offered comments. Final revisions were then made.

Factors Considered in These Reviews

Each test was reviewed according to the following guidelines and criteria:*

---

*This monograph cannot explore these criteria in depth nor their importance. The International Reading Association has published a monograph which treats these topics in a style understandable by educators without any background in measurement. Readers interested in more information about these topics should consult Schreiner, Robert, editor. *Reading tests and teachers: A practical guide.* Newark, Delaware: International Reading Association, 1979.

Description of contents
Test development
Aspects of validity
Aspects of reliability
Administration and scoring
The manual

For several reasons it was impossible to evaluate most of the tests in this monograph according to all of the usual test-evaluation criteria. Not all of the tests were developed and/or standardized using traditional procedures; therefore, some data usually relied upon by test reviewers was unavailable. Also, in several instances, communications with the publisher failed to produce data said or implied to have been used in developing a test. In these instances, reviewers had to rely upon their preceptions and informed opinion rather than upon theoretical constructs and/or numerical data. As a result, some aspects of these reviews are not as incisive or as conclusive as readers may desire them to be.

Test Development

There are recommended procedures for developing a test and the closer these are adhered to, the better the test will be. Test manuals should contain sufficiently detailed information to permit the prospective user to decide accurately how well these recommendations were followed. Some questions to which answers should be available are: How were passages and items selected? Was there a tryout followed by a revision? If standardized, was the norm group adequate and representative? If criterion-referenced, how were the criteria determined?

How scores were determined is a very important part of test development. Standardized tests use derived scores such as grade equivalents, percentile ranks, and stanines, all expressed in numerals. These scores are based on a "norm" or standardization group. The degree to which this norm group meets certain criteria determines, in part, the precision of the scores and the confidence we can have in them.

There is no single way in which the scores of criterion-referenced tests are determined. Some test constructors feel that external criteria can be set, e.g., 75 percent, 90 percent, etc., against which a student's performance can be compared.

Whether this is sound is quite controversial. For reasons too complicated to discuss here, some educators feel that it's neither sound nor possible to set external criteria (Glass, 1978). On the other hand, some tests labeled criterion-referenced provide normative data—how one student compares with the norm group, as well as how the student fared in relation to the external criteria used with the test. Criterion-referenced tests which don't base their criteria upon actual performance of previous test-takers need to be rigorously scrutinized to insure that their criteria are sound, realistic, and feasible; these standards should not be blindly accepted.

Hayward (1968) points out that if scores on subtests are to be differentially useful, each subtest should be relatively independent of the other subtests. Correlation coefficients between subtests should be low, below .65. The lower the correlation between subscores, the more likely it is that they are measuring different things.* The higher the correlation, the more likely it is that they are measuring the same thing. Therefore, if subscores are to be used to group students for instruction, low subtest intercorrelations are desirable.

Most published survey tests of reading achievement, such as Metropolitan Reading Tests, Iowa Tests of Basic Skills, Gates-MacGinitie Reading Tests, etc., have been adequately constructed and standardized. Therefore, educators may overgeneralize and expect *all* reading tests to have been similarly produced. Since this is not the case—as some reviews herein show—educators should read the test development section of the review with more than passing interest.

Validity

Test validity refers to how well an instrument measures what it is being used to measure. With diagnostic and criterion-referenced instruments, it is crucial that the test or subtest measure only or primarily what it is designed to measure. For example, a subtest labeled "Decoding" should primarily

---

*The reliability of subtests also strongly influences the correlation between these subtests. Two generally unreliable subtests will be less highly correlated than if both were more reliable. Therefore, only when individual subtest reliabilities are high, in the upper 80s or above, will low subtest correlations indicate that they are measuring different things.

Schell

measure a reader's ability to translate printed symbols into the sounds they represent. This can be accomplished in several acceptable ways, but the results should not be contaminated to any large degree by examinee knowledge of factors such as sight words, word meanings, names of pictures, etc. To the degree that these factors are present, the test becomes invalid. For numerous reasons it is impossible to construct "pure" tests of reading skills, ones that measure only one factor each. But the closer a subtest comes to eliminating irrelevant factors, the more confidence we can have in the meaning and interpretation of its results.

The reason validity is so crucial is that invalid tests give invalid results which in turn may lead to either unnecessary instruction or lack of needed instruction. We are not interested in validity for its own sake; we are interested in it because test results are frequently used to determine subsequent instruction. This requires valid, not questionable, information. The section in these reviews on validity deserves special attention by readers.

In reviewing the tests, assessing validity of the various subtests was difficult for several reasons. First, several of the test manuals provided only partial validity information, and others provided none. In such cases, educators are being asked to trust the test's author(s). Experience has shown that information is a better guide in judging test validity than is faith. Absence or inadequacy of validity information should raise some fundamental questions about a test.

Second, since there is no professional consensus as to the various skills in reading, no two tests include identical subtests. In fact, several tests reviewed herein for the same reading level were more different than alike. Finally, assessing validity was complicated by the fact that numerous procedures have been used to measure the same stated skill. In some tests, examinees choose from among multiple choice responses; in others, they produce an oral response. Some tests include pictures, others letters, and still others words to measure an identically-named skill. These idiosyncratic aspects, coupled with the lack of definite standards against which to judge the tests, often made it difficult for reviewers to know exactly what the tests measure or whether they measure what they purport to measure.

An example of a common validity problem in the tests reviewed was how decoding is assessed. In group tests, the examiner commonly pronounces a word and the examinee is asked to circle or write a letter or group of letters representing a sound somewhere in the word. It has been argued that this is encoding, or spelling, *not* decoding. In reading, when confronted with an unrecognized word, the reader says or thinks the sounds represented by the letters, a process generally the reverse of that used in group diagnostic tests. The question for the test evaluator then is, "Is selecting (writing) a letter for a heard sound the same as, or essentially equivalent to, saying or thinking a sound when confronted by the letter representing it?" In other words, will an *encoding* test give valid *decoding* information? Pikulski and Shanahan (1980) doubt that it will.

Reliability

Test reliability refers to the accuracy and consistency of test results. Reliability is important because it indicates how much confidence we can place in the accuracy of a test's results. The more reliable a test, the more faith we have that, if tested again with the same or a different form of that test, a student's or a group's score will be similar in both testings. In conventional standardized achievement tests, reliability is expressed as a numerical coefficient, e.g., .72, .89, etc., which indicates how much confidence we can have in the score and how much error is present. Most standardized reading tests have reliabilities from .85 to .96. The higher the correlation, the less error the test probably contains.

Conventional procedures for determining reliability require variability in scores, that is, a range of scores so that it can be determined whether scores are consistently high or low in retest situations. But several tests reviewed in this monograph were deliberately constructed to produce low interpupil variability. That is, nearly all examinees "pass" the test (meet the standards set by the test's authors). Therefore, procedures other than conventional data analyses had to be used by reviewers in evaluating the reliability of some of the tests.

General factors that make a test reliable are test length or the number of items measuring an objective. When passages are longer in an oral reading test or when there are more items measuring an objective, the test tends to be more reliable. The reliability of a test using only one, two, or three items to measure an objective or in which a pupil reads only 10 words in a word list is probably lower than desirable. Especially in multiple-choice tests where guessing is possible, a few items cannot unequivocally indicate whether an examinee possesses the stated competence.

In the absence of reliability data, educators need to examine how many items measure each objective or skill, the length of word lists and passages, and what the examinee's chances of guessing the right answer are.

Ease of Administration and Scoring

Giving, scoring, and interpreting the test should require reasonable amounts of time. Also, procedures for all three of these tasks should be relatively straightforward and conventional. If they are not, they are likely to engender confusion, error, misuse, and teacher cynicism about the value of testing.

The Manual

The manual should clearly and forthrightly deal with the four aspects discussed above: 1) test development; 2) validity; 3) reliability; and 4) administration, scoring, and interpretation. This information should be provided in sufficient detail and clarity for potential users to judge the appropriateness of the test for their purposes. Many manuals also pinpoint unique features of the test as well as its limitations. A quality manual is essential, not merely a nicety.

Other Factors to Consider in Selecting and Interpreting a Test

The purpose for which the test is to be given should be clearly and accurately specified by the test administrator before administration. Test results should help educators make wise and salutary decisions, not merely be recorded and forgotten in cumulative folders or governmental reports. Educators who don't know why they are using a test will likely gather inappropriate information, waste their students' and their own time, and possibly give inappropriate instruction based on the results—hardly the acts of a professional. This fundamental step of knowing why the test is being given or what use will be made should not be ignored.

A factor that complicates the selection and interpretation of a diagnostic and/or criterion-referenced test that can't be reviewed in a publication like this is the user's notions or beliefs about reading. There is a great controversy among reading educators as to whether reading is primarily a global, unitary entity or one comprised of numerous discrete subskills. Those who hold the former belief may be uncomfortable with many of the tests and reviews in this book because they disagree that reading can be fractionated in these ways or that these are the most important skills and processes to be diagnosed. Other educators have no such qualms and will find that many of these tests mirror their assumptions about what reading is and how it should be measured and taught. The point is that tests, in and of themselves, may not necessarily be good or bad, appropriate or inappropriate. Rather, one's point of view as to what constitutes reading and reading instruction may ultimately be more important in evaluating and choosing a test than is the test itself. This requires test users to determine what they believe reading and reading instruction are and then to choose a test that best matches this definition rather than merely comparing one test with another.

Also, the test user's professional competence must be candidly assessed. Some tests require only that directions be read and answers objectively scored while others require subjective decisions that can be made best by educators with much professional preparation and experience in teaching and testing children. Educators should not choose a test whose demands exceed their competency to give, score, or interpret it.

Last, the results of *all* tests are intended to be interpreted along with other information, not in isolation. Teacher observations, student work samples, parental interviews, previous test results, insights from other professionals, etc. should all be combined to give a larger, more accurate, and usable picture than that available from the test results alone. Test results can be most beneficial if used in this way.

What is the Responsibility of Test Publishers?

The following quote from a previous IRA monograph reviewing reading tests (Blanton, Farr, & Tuinman, 1972) cannot be improved upon.

> A test should be placed in the same category as a critical drug. A test should be used only after a careful study of its effects has been made. Evidence should be provided that the test (or drug) will do what it purports to do. Too many critical decisions are made about a child based on his test scores to use any test that is not a reliable and valid assessment of his ability to do the task described by the test. A teacher should insist that the test manufacturers provide him with the same reputable product that he would demand of a drug manufacturer who offers a new cure. It is better to use no test than to use an unreliable or invalid one. One finds that a number of tests are released before adequate data are available.

Many tests have not been studied sufficiently before they are put on the market for sale. One hopes the reader will note these deficiencies and realize how serious the action is to make an instructional, promotional, or evaluational decision about a child when it is not based on an accurate, stable, or predictive measure of his achievement.

Selecting a reading achievement test is a complex task. Many tests are available, yet evaluating even a single test requires more time than most educators have. This is particularly true of diagnostic and criterion-referenced tests which often, for various reasons, can't be evaluated quickly and easily as this introduction has tried to point out. These test reviews are offered to educators as an aid in their efforts to select the most appropriate test for their specific needs.

References

Blanton, William, Farr, Roger, & Tuinman, J. Jaap. *Reading tests for the secondary grades: A review and evaluation.* Newark, Delaware: International Reading Association, 1972, 7.

Buros, Oscar. *Seventh mental measurements yearbook.* Highland Park, New Jersey: Gryphon, 1972, xxvii.

Buros, Oscar. *Eighth mental measurements yearbook.* Highland Park, New Jersey: Gryphon, 1978.

Glass, Gene. Standards and criteria. *Journal of Educational Measurement, 15* (Winter 1978), 237-261.

Hayward, Priscilla. Evaluating diagnostic reading tests. *Reading Teacher, 21* (March 1968), 237-261.

Pikulski, John, & Shanahan, Timothy. A comparison of various approaches to evaluating phonics. *Reading Teacher, 33* (March 1980), 692-702.

Popham, W. James. Well-crafted criterion-referenced tests. *Educational Leadership, 36* (November 1978), 91-95.

Schell, Leo M. Criterion-referenced reading tests: Some cautionary notes. *Reading World, 19* (October 1979), 57-62.

Test Reviews

Individual Tests

Botel Reading Inventory

Edition   Second
Author   Morton Botel
Publisher Follett Publishing Company
Company   1978
Reviewer   Jane Warren Meeks, Old Dominion University
Critiquers Robert Carvell, University of Kansas, and Leo M.
           Schell, Kansas State University

Overview

The Botel Reading Inventory (BRI) is an informal test that can be easily administered in the classroom. It consists of four separate tests: the Decoding Test, Spelling Placement Test, Word Recognition Test (Forms A and B) and Word Opposites Test (Forms A and B). All tests are termed "power tests" because there are no time limits. Test items consist of isolated words; there are no passages or paragraphs to be read.

The Word Recognition Test and the Word Opposite Test comprise what Botel terms the Reading Placement Tests. They are intended to help teachers place students at their instructional levels in basal readers. The results indicate three levels of reading competency, 1) free reading level, 2) instructional level, and 3) frustration level, and one level of reading potential. The primary scoring objective is to find the student's highest instructional level on all tests. The criteria for instructional placement are: 1) the student recognizes and pronounces 70-90 percent of the words on the Word Recognition Test and 2) the student scores 70-80 percent on the items in the

Word Opposites Test. No explanation is given as to how these criteria were established.

The Decoding Tests consist of 12 subtests comprising 7 levels ranging from awareness of sounds and letter correspondences to decoding multi-syllabic nonsense words. Each subtest consists of ten items. The first three subtests may be administered on a group basis while subtests 4-12 must be administered individually. Subtests 4-12 are word lists based upon selected phonic and syllabic principles. The error marking procedures for subtests 4-12 (Decoding Syllable/Spelling Patterns) of mispronunciation, substitution, and lack of response are adequate for classroom use but would prevent a more detailed analysis sometimes desired by clinicians. The author, aware of regional and dialectical pronunciation differences, tells teachers to allow for such differences and to count them as correct. There is not a single word in the manual explaining how the results are to be used.

The purpose of the Spelling Placement Test is to give an estimate of the grade level at which a student should be placed for spelling instruction. The test consists of five graded lists of 20 words each (grades 1 and 2 being combined) which were sampled at random from the author's spelling series. This test is probably minimally valid *only* for use with the series from which the words were selected (Follett, 1975) and should definitely not be used for placement in other series. Why it is included in this inventory is very unclear.

The Word Recognition Test (Forms A and B) is administered individually and is designed to yield an estimate of oral reading ability. The test is comprised of eight 20-word samples from the preprimer level through fourth grade. Thus, this test is of limited usefulness for students reading above fourth grade level. The author states that the words were selected from five major basal readers although no specific titles are given. From information available in the manual, it appears that the words were generated from a study conducted in 1968. They seem not to have been updated for the 1978 edition of this test. The testing is to be continued until the student falls below 70 percent on two successive levels.

The Word Opposites Test (Forms A and B), an estimate of comprehension, is administered on a group basis. It appears that this test might be more accurately interpreted as a measure of word knowledge. The ten-word subtests include first reader level through senior high school. One composite list is designed for Junior High (grades 7-9) and for Senior High (grades 10-12), so that no explicit information can be gleaned for secondary placement in textbooks or for grouping considertions. The manual also indicates that this test will yield a reading potential level when read orally to the student. Testing is discontinued when the student falls below 80 percent on two successive levels. Criteria on these tests are similar to those of an informal inventory. Thus, teachers familiar with them can draw interpretive conclusions from these scores.

Interpreting Results

Interpreting the results is not necessarily a simple matter, as Botel recognizes that for many students the instructional level is not a single level but rather a range of levels at which they can read with profit. While reflecting reality, this fact complicates the interpretation of results and may frequently cause the test administrator to have to choose an instructional level from among several scores. Examples are given in the manual, but they are not always as clear as one would like, nor is the author's rationale for choosing among competing scores lucidly explained. Care should be exercised by teachers unfamiliar with interpreting the results of the Word Recognition and Word Opposites tests.

Fortunately the author does emphasize that the results are only estimates of the instructional level and that subsequent evaluation will also be needed.

Norms

At first, because this is essentially a criterion-referenced test, the complete lack of norms isn't troubling. But without some such data, it is impossible to determine whether the author's stated criteria, e.g., 70-80 percent correct on the Word Opposite Test, are valid or realistic. Some of these data are contained incidentally in tables that are intended for other purposes but none are presented forthrightly. Faith in the test's criteria could have been substantially improved if such information had been provided.

Reliability

While the manual reports correlation between test forms, it does not specify whether this is for a subtest score (and if so, which one) or for a total score. Because of this lack of information, the coefficients purporting to show the relationship between forms A and B should be viewed skeptically.

No reliability data are given for any subtests, making it impossible to determine the amount of error likely to be in a given score. Neither are any test-retest reliability data given.

Validity

Three types of validity—content, criterion-related, and concurrent—are discussed in the manual. In content validity, the rationale for why vocabulary items were chosen to represent oral reading fluency and silent reading comprehension is essentially that vocabulary blends word recognition (pronunciation) and word meaning with simplicity and objectivity for classroom teachers in estimating students' instructional level in basal readers.

Two studies are reported to show that the BRI is valid for placing students in basal readers at their instructional levels (criterion-related validity). Correlations, apparently between the BRI's, Word Recognition and Word Opposites tests, and teacher placement in basal readers, are respectable for grades 2 through 5 (.77-.95) but less impressive for grades 1 and 6, apparently indicating that caution should be exercised in using the BRI in these grades. This conclusion is substantiated by the steady decline in correlation between the BRI and standardized silent reading tests from an impressive high of .92 in grade 2 to an unimpressive .63 in grade 5 and a questionable .51 in grade 6.

The second study was a complicated one involving comparison of the Botel and three oral reading inventories. Even though superficially impressive, because of the well-known problems of scoring error and low inter-scorer reliability on oral reading tests (neither of which is acknowledged or reported in the BRI manual), these figures should not be taken literally but rather as an indication that the BRI generally measures the same things as do tests requiring oral reading of paragraphs.

One very troubling aspect of reported validity and reliability data is that they were determined using the 1970 edition. Thus the data may tell us about previous editions rather than this one.

Conclusions

1. The BRI is a moderately useful inventory for a classroom teacher to use to place children at their instructional levels in basal readers. Care should be exercised in interpreting the results, and other information should be collected to confirm or reject the results of this inventory.

2. It is much more powerful in grades 2 and 3 than in grades 4 and 5, and there are serious problems with its use in grade 6.

3. Little faith should be placed in the ability of the spelling subtest to place students accurately in a spelling program, which is the stated purpose of the test.

4. Since no information is given on its interpretation, the Decoding Test should be given only by teachers thoroughly familiar with and experienced in teaching these skills. Others should avoid it.

5. The lack of passages makes the results yield only as much information as does a modified graded word list. With the strong current emphasis on syntactic and semantic cues and on reading comprehension, the BRI's lack of tests for reading and understanding connected discourse may make it unacceptable to educators interested in these aspects of reading development.

6. Because no data or explanations are given to support either the concept or the determination of the reading potential level, it seems best if this level is not calculated from the results from the BRI.

Classroom Reading Inventory

Edition   Third
Author   Nicholas J. Silvaroli
Publisher Wm. C. Brown Company
Copyright 1976
Reviewer Ozeal Shyne Brown, Washington D.C. Public
            Schools
Critiquers Kitte Phillips, California State College at Fullerton
            and Clyde G. Colwell, Kansas State University

Overview

The third edition of the Classroom Reading Inventory (CRI) is a diagnostic instrument intended to provide a relatively quick (approximately 12 minutes) indication of a student's reading level, preprimer through grade 8. From the CRI the examiner can obtain information about levels of reading (independent, instructional, frustration, and hearing capacity) as well as some indication of word recognition and comprehension strengths and weaknesses. In addition, spelling skills can be assessed by this instrument.

The inventory assesses three aspects of reading: 1) recognition of words in isolation, 2) oral reading (word recognition and comprehension), and 3) spelling. All components needed for the test are contained within one spiral booklet—examiner directions, student selections, and the examiner's copy of the reading/testing sections. The pages are perforated and punched to fit a three-ring notebook. In that way, examiner materials and directions can be separated from the student sections and placed in different notebooks. Since the publisher allows reproduction of all pages that would normally be marked by the examiner, expenditures for CRI test materials are minimized.

The CRI test booklet contains three forms (A, B, and C) and each form is composed of three sections: Part I-Graded Word Lists, Part II-Oral Selections, and Part III-Spelling Surveys. Parts I and II of each form are intended to be individual measures, while Part III may be used in group testing. Silvaroli proposes that Form A selections be read orally and Form B selections be read silently so that a more complete profile can be developed. The examiner could then read Form C to the student to establish the hearing capacity level.

The range of reading selections (Part II) on any of the forms is preprimer through grade 8. The graded word lists (Part I) and the spelling surveys (Part III) extended from preprimer through sixth grade. The graded word lists contain 20 words at each level while the spelling surveys include 10 words per level. The oral reading selections vary in length (from 24 to 174 words per selection) and each is followed by five comprehension questions. For added motivation, each passage is illustrated and the examiner is provided with a purpose-setting statement for each individual selection.

Critical Discussion

It appears, in general terms, that the author has satisfied many of his stated purposes: The CRI can be administered in a comparatively short time and the degree of training needed to administer and interpret the test is not extensive. In short, the CRI may represent a viable means by which a classroom teacher can gain more diagnostic information than that which is usually available from the score of a standardized survey test. The motivational statements and the illustrations may make the test more palatable to the students. An unstated value may be that when elementary students are to be instructed from a wide array of reading materials, it may be best to administer a "neutral" informal reading inventory, such as the CRI, as opposed to one accompanying a particular basal reading series.

The CRI also has many characteristics that may be viewed as serious limitations. Perhaps the most obvious concern is that no reliability or validity data are reported in the test manual. A test that yields stable or consistent scores is a reliable test. Will Johnny's performance be consistent when measured more than once by the CRI? An estimate of reliability could have been provided by testing individuals with Form A and at a later time with Form B. The more highly the two sets of scores correlate, the greater the reliability of the parallel forms. The CRI does not provide this type of information.

Validity is an equally important issue. Simply stated, the concern is, "Does the test measure what it is intended to measure?" Silvaroli offers no evidence of *content validity* (the appropriateness of the oral passages, comprehension items, or the suitability of the spelling items) other than to mention that the passages (sources unknown) were screened via several readability measures. Also, no *concurrent validity* is reported. A degree of concurrent validity would be established by comparing a set of performances on the CRI to performances by the same individuals on a similar test. The examiner may wish to know to what extent the instructional level on the CRI predicts successful performance in a comparable level basal reader. For this, some measure of *predictive validity* should be established and presented in the manual.

The central issue is not necessarily what type of reliability and validity should be furnished; the key issue is that no empirical data are given in the manual. These types of data must be presented so that teachers and reading specialists know whether the results are meaningful and generalizable, or simply arbitrary constructs established by one person.

Neither is any evidence presented to justify the assumption that if the hearing capacity level is higher than the child's instuctional level, the child's reading skills may be improved, at least to this level, through further instruction. This reasoning would make most children appear to need remedial instruction, since the auditory comprehension of nearly all first through third graders far exceeds their reading comprehension. Professional educators should view with caution unsupported statements about the relationship between listening and reading.

Another facet of the CRI that should be scrutinized carefully is the manner in which specific types of comprehension questions are collectively proportioned. An analysis of all three forms of the CRI indicates (in rounded numbers) that 56 percent of the questions are factual, 29 percent inferential, and 15 percent vocabulary (word meaning). These percentages are present if Silvaroli's labels are accepted for all comprehension items. It is possible, for example, for the examinee to begin taking the CRI at the preprimer level (Form B, Part II) and continue through the fifth reader level and encounter only three vocabulary questions. In any form of the CRI, extending from preprimer through eighth grade, there are not enough vocabulary items to adequately measure that skill (total vocabulary questions: Form A = 8, Form B = 7, and Form C = 7).

Also, the types of comprehension questions following individual selections vary dramatically. For example, Form B, level 5 contains four factual, one inferential, and no vocabulary questions. Form C, level 6 has one factual, three inferential, and one vocabulary question. Without some consistency or format patterning from level to level, one can never be sure what the results indicate. The variance in question type and the paucity of vocabulary questions makes level-setting tenuous at best and inaccurate at worst.

Another concern with the comprehension sections is that certain specific weaknesses in previous editions of the CRI, as delineated by Spache (1976), are still present. Spache pointed out that some inference questions really measure reader background and are not answerable by reading passage, and other questions labeled as "inference" are actually literal. (See Spache, 1976, pp. 181-183, for specific questions.)

Some scoring procedures are ambiguous. A typical example is found in Form C, Part II, level 5. The scoring guide delineates the levels as follows:

Word Recognition Errors		Comprehension Errors
Independent	2	0-1
Instructional	6	1½-2
Frustration	11½	2½+

What level would be assigned if a student missed five words? Or ten words? It must be assumed, in such cases, that Silvaroli is allowing the examiner some discretion. If so, it's a type of discretion that is not provided uniformly at each level. In reference to comprehension, it can be noted from the scoring guide that 1½ to 2 mistakes are permissible (out of 5 questions) for the student to be considered at his/her instructional level. The instructional level comprehension figures (1½-2) are consistent at all levels. One might thus conclude that 60-70 percent is equated with instructional level. Yet, in the manual (p. xii), Silvaroli defines instructional level as 75 percent comprehension. Does 60 percent comprehension predict success in the classroom? Without supporting data, it can only be assumed that this is an arbitrary standard.

The "Inventory Record" needs to be used judiciously. It encourages judgments to be made about specific word recognition and comprehension deficiencies on the basis of errors made in oral reading and in answering questions. Experts in educational measurement seriously question whether these kinds of decisions can be validly and reliably made based on the analysis of such data.

Conclusions

The major advantages of the third edition of the CRI are that it represents a reasonably practical way for a classroom teacher to gain some added insights about individual student performance.

The CRI is a gross screening (or placement) device that is neither designed for nor adequate as a more complete diagnostic assessment.

In the absence of reliability and validity information, the examiner must remain skeptical about the test construction and the meaningfulness of the level-setting criteria. At present, one is forced to assume that the test format and placement standards are arbitrary.

When interpreting results from the CRI, the examiner should carefully judge whether enough items have been included to measure a specific skill (i.e., vocabulary-type comprehension) and whether the skill category (i.e., inferential-type comprehension) was properly labeled by the author.

There is little consistency or patterning between levels of question type and passage length. This lack of internal structuring not only raises doubts about the accuracy of level-setting, but also greatly reduces any chances for item analysis of the questions.

Reference

Spache, George D. *Diagnosing and correcting reading disabilities.* Boston: Allyn and Bacon, 1976, 181-183.

Diagnostic Reading Scales

Edition   Second
Author   George D. Spache
Publisher CTB/McGraw-Hill
Copyright 1972
Reviewer   Peter Mosenthal, State University of New York at
           Albany
Critiquer Shirley Jackson, U.S. Department of Education,
           Washington, D.C.

Overview

Overall, the test assesses three levels of reading ability of elementary school pupils and remedial secondary school readers: instructional, independent, and potential reading levels. In addition, the test determines patterns of reading skill development, including word attack, word analysis, sight recognition, and auditory discrimination. The scales consist of three word recognition lists, each graduated in difficulty, and two reading passages for each of the eleven levels. The levels range from first to eighth grade. The final section of the test consists of eight supplementary phonics tests. Administration of the total test takes about 45 minutes.

The word recognition score is based on one of three word lists, each consisting of 40 to 50 words. Word recognition norms provide grade level scores from 1.3 to 6.5. The principal use of the word lists is to provide an estimate of which passage the child should be able to read in the second part of the test and where to begin in this testing. The lists also are intended to provide insight into how a student analyzes words and how she or he recognizes sight words in isolation. In scoring this section of the test, only words correctly pronounced upon immediate presentation are counted correct. Words correctly pronounced after a few seconds are counted as errors both in scoring and in determining when to stop testing.

In determining a child's oral reading ability, two scores from the passages are used: 1) the number of questions correctly answered, and 2) the number of oral reading errors made. Oral reading errors include omissions, additions, substitutions or mispronunciations, repetitions, reversals, and aided words. The oral reading level is determined by the highest-level selection a child can read a) with no more than the average number of errors for children at that reading level and b) with no less than 60 percent comprehension of seven or eight questions, both literal and inferential, which follow each passage. The latter represents a departure from the traditional criterion of 75 percent on comprehension, which must be kept in mind when the results of this test are compared with more usual determinations of reading level.

The procedure used to identify a child's instructional level is as follows. If the child fails the first passage tried, either in oral reading errors or comprehension, the child is dropped back to the passage of the next lower readability level. Or, if the child passes the first passage, she or he continues with successive trial passages, each at a half or full grade level higher, to the point where the failure in oral reading errors or comprehension occurs. The instructional level is the passage immediately below the point of failure.

Silent reading is measured on this test in a format separate from, but intergral to, the measurement of oral reading. When the reader has failed to meet the criteria for oral reading, she or he is given silent reading passages starting at the next higher level of difficulty and asked to read them silently. The highest passage in which the reader can meet or exceed the 60 percent comprehension criterion is then taken to be the silent reading level. In a departure from the usual designations, Spache refers to this level as the independent reading level—the highest level at which a reader can read silently with adequate comprehension. For many of the pupils tested with this instrument, the independent reading level will be at a higher level than the instructional level. The more conventional practice has been to designate an independent reading level which is easier than instructional level. Users of this test will have to determine whether Spache's position on the independent reading level is compatible with their own opinions as to the relative placement of this level.

An auditory comprehension portion of the test is used to measure reading potential. For this segment, the tester reads the passages aloud to the pupil at a level just above the child's independent level. The highest passage level a child is able to comprehend with 60 percent accuracy is said to be the level of material a child could read if she or he were experiencing no reading difficulties.

The final section of this test consists of eight supplementary phonics tests which measure, in isolation, the reader's ability to use skills which are generally representative of a synthetic phonics program. These tests include tests of consonant sounds, vowel sounds, consonant blends and digraphs, common syllables or phonograms, blending, letter sounds, initial consonant substitution, and auditory discrimination. These subtests present the skills in a straightforward but isolated fashion, with all the uncertainty of interpretation that can be expected from such isolation. However, this isolation does prevent the measurement from being contaminated by other extraneous factors.

Test Development

Apparently the Scales, particularly the passages, were developed, tried out, and revised informally over an extended period of time prior to the standardization administration. Thus, some explanations about their construction are vague, undocumented, and difficult to assess.

Procedures other than merely using readability formulas were used to establish accuracy of reading level. Passage levels are probably more accurate than in similar tests but their precision cannot be vouched for.

The standards determining whether a student passes a passage were obtained from test results of 2,000 children, a minimum of 100 at each reading level. Mean errors for oral reading, oral comprehension, and silent comprehension were calculated and standards for the passages arbitrarily determined from these. It appears that only the 1963 edition was tried out, not the 1972 edition.

Even though better constructed than similar tests and even though an abundance of tryout data is available, because of some unpresented data and some unclear explanations, users should interpret scores obtained on the Scales somewhat more cautiously than they would those obtained from standardized silent reading tests but with more confidence than they do those from similar placement tests.

Reliability

Even though unclear on some points, reliability data are impressive, at least in terms of quantity. Word lists are highly reliable, .87 to .96, even though it is pointed out that these correlations may be slightly high because of how the test is administered and because the sample upon which they are based was quite heterogeneous.

Passage reliability coefficients of .84 to .88 are reported for a ten-week test-retest period. However, no details are reported, so it is impossible to interpret these data. Based on a five-month test-retest period, stability coefficients ranging from .79 to .88 are reported for the Instructional Level while the Potential Level yielded coefficients of .67 to .94. These data, although not conclusive, coupled with experience in using the test, lead the reviewers to believe that it is one of the more reliable oral reading tests available, reliable enough to use before and after instruction to measure growth.

The standard errors of measurement, a function of list and passage reliability, are also reported and seem small enough to give users confidence that obtained scores are generally—although not exactly—accurate.

Validity

Words selected for the word recognition tests were chosen on the basis of adequate discrimination and appropriate difficulty. Estimates of predictive validity (.65 to .78, using Instructional Level as criterion) are sufficiently high to justify using the lists to determine which reading passage to begin with.

Content validity, the materials used in the passages, seems quite adequate. Construct validity, determined in several ways, is not quite as impressive. During the test's construction, students read a selection from the Scales and a parallel selection from a similar test. Proposed passages that didn't demonstrate validity were replaced by more valid passages. It is also reported that the Instructional Levels were constantly compared with the teacher's judgments of their students' reading levels and, if frequent discrepancies were found, revisions were made in the passages. The lack of details somewhat weakens the author's case for the accuracy of the passages. Using the passages for placement may only be generally accurate, not exactly so.

Concurrent validity was determined by comparing performance on the Scales with that on both oral and silent reading tests and with teacher judgment. The Scales correlated .90 with three other oral reading tests, and their Instructional Levels correlated from .67 to .87 with a silent reading test. In one study of 56 children, there was a higher percentage of agreement between the Scales and teacher judgment than between the Scales and a silent reading test. The conclusion was that the Scales would be more nearly adequate in placing children into instructional material than silent reading tests would be. No similar test has anywhere near this amount of concurrent validity data. But it is clearly only approximate, not exact and conclusive.

Potential Level

As with all predictions of potential reading ability, this seemingly straightforward technique has two major faults. One, listening comprehension does not represent a fixed ability; it is amenable to improvement with direct instruction. Therefore, a child without training in listening, who shows no difference between his or her potential and instructional level could be falsely labeled as reading at capacity (and hence not a candidate for special help in reading).

Second, a more serious problem is that there is little conclusive evidence available to indicate that auditory comprehension adequately predicts potential reading level, particularly for primary grade children. As suggested by Table 15 in the Examiner's Manual, this test's potential level grossly overestimates the actual potential level of children in first and second grade, and possibly even in third. The discrepancy between potential level means the actual grade placement shown is so great that the children, as a group, surely could not have been reading that far below their capabilities. This point is also supported by the Technical Bulletin where the reading potential level so far exceeds grade placement as to make it suspect. In addition to these observations, common sense and experiences suggest that auding will far exceed ability during first, second, and possibly even third grade. For example, it is easy to imagine a group of first graders in January comprehending 60 percent of third to fifth grade level material read to them. Measuring potential level of primary grade pupils would make most of them appear to be candidates for remedial reading instruction. Therefore, the Potential Level should be interpreted with far more caution even than the manual suggests.

Phonic Tests

The phonic tests are criterion-referenced—even though grade scores are provided. It is stated in the manual that these scores are only estimates of where the skills are typically taught and that the tests are only intended to provide specific clues to instructional needs of students. Further comparison with the regular reading program's placement of these skills is encouraged, but there is no real information as how to interpret these tests. Therefore, cautious use and interpretation are recommended.

Conclusions

The Diagnostic Reading Scales represent an individually administered reading test that is relatively well constructed, although not with the rigor which is characteristic of group silent reading tests. This lessens the degree of confidence that can be placed in the results. The philosophical background for the development of the instrument represents a modified traditional stance: Traditional in the sense that a) skills are measured because they are usually taught, b) reading achievement levels are based on oral reading, and c) reading potential is defined as listening comprehension. The basic modification of traditional practice occurs in two areas. First, adequate comprehension throughout the instrument is defined as 60 percent rather than as the traditional 75 percent; and, second, independent reading level is defined as meeting the 60 percent criterion in silent reading comprehension rather than the more usual 90 percent criterion with near perfect pronunciation in oral reading. The value of the use of the Scales lies in the user's acceptance of these positions.

Durrell Analysis of Reading Difficulty

Author   Donald D. Durrell
Publisher Harcourt Brace Jovanovich
Copyright 1955
Reviewer   Dolly Cinquino, Glen Rock, New Jersey, Public Schools
Critiquer Robert E. Jennings, Ft. Hays State University

Overview

The Durrell Analysis of Reading Difficulty is a well-known test frequently used by classroom teachers and reading specialists. It was designed to observe the reading performance of children ranging from nonreaders to those reading on the sixth grade level. It is a hand-scorable test which must be administered individually and requires thirty to ninety minutes of testing time, depending on the selection of subtests.

According to the description in the Manual, "the primary purpose of the Analysis is to discover weaknesses and faulty habits in reading which may be corrected in a remedial program." The Oral Reading, Silent Reading, and Listening Comprehension Tests form the core of the Analysis. The Oral Reading Test includes eight graded paragraphs, comprehension questions, checklists for observing difficulties, and norms. The Silent Reading Test contains eight paragraphs "equal in difficulty to the oral reading paragraphs," a form for recording unaided and aided oral recall, checklists for observing difficulties, questions for checking imagery, and norms. The Listening Comprehension Tests include seven graded paragraphs and comprehension questions. Supplementary graded paragraphs are provided for further testing.

The other parts of the Analysis include tests of decoding and encoding skills. The Word Recognition and Word Analysis

Test includes word cards and a tachistoscope. Two word lists are given, one for grade one, and another for grades two to six. Separate norms and checklists for recognition and analysis and a phonics inventory for the primary grades are also included. The Visual Memory of Word Forms, Auditory Analysis of Word Elements, and Spelling and Handwriting Tests each consists of two subtests, one for the primary and one for the intermediate grades.

Additionally, the manual includes: Suggestions for Supplementary Tests and Observations, Profile Chart, Checklist of Instructional Needs, General History Forms, and Special Tests for the Nonreader on the Preprimer Reader.

The directions for administering the tests are clear and easy to follow and emphasize the importance of observing difficulties the reader may be having. Experience is necessary to administer the tests in order to record all errors correctly and to provide a smooth flow in the testing situation, particularly when using the tachistoscope. The manual suggests that the Oral Reading Tests be given first because the selection of the other tests to be administered depends upon the reading level obtained in the oral tests. However, there is no fixed order to administering the tests.

Technical Aspects

Norms for each grade, divided into high, middle, and low, are provided for the Oral Reading Tests, the Silent Reading Tests, and the Word Recognition and Word Analysis Tests. Rough grade equivalents are given for scores on the other tests. According to the Manual the norm tables "are based on no fewer than a thousand children for each test." There is no further information about the norming population. Further data regarding standardization procedures is glaringly omitted. The oral reading norms are based solely on reading speed. Silent reading norms make use of reading rate and the number of "memories" from reading.

The publisher also maintains that "In the extensive use of these tests, the norms have been found to check satisfactorily against other measures of reading ability." This claim of concurrent validity lacks support. The reliability and validity of the Analysis are highly questionable in the light of such limited data.

Description and Evaluation of Subtests
Reading/Listening Sections

The Oral Reading Tests consist of timed reading of several short paragraphs sequentially listed by grade level. Administration requires practice because quick and careful notations must be made of several different kinds of errors. Although the Manual stresses the importance of evaluating errors to assess weaknesses in the child's reading, the emphasis here is on the speed at which the child completes the paragraphs. Comprehension questions require low level responses and refer to specific items in the text. No norms are established for the comprehension questions and it appears that if the child can decode, he or she will probably be able to answer most of the questions because they require simple recall of the text. Because the Oral Reading Tests place emphasis on measuring reading speed and ability to recall explicitly stated information, their value in assessing comprehension skills is limited. Current research reveals the need to examine the types of errors the reader makes in order to understand the child's processing of print. This battery of tests does not call for that kind of careful analysis of comprehension.

The Silent Reading Tests are basically the same as the Oral Reading Tests with norms given for the timed reading of eight paragraphs. Comprehension is tested by having the child recall as much of the paragraph read as possible. The measure of comprehension is a checklist of the "memories" immediately recalled by the child and therefore stresses simple factual recall. No specific questions are given. The examiner is directed to question children who cannot spontaneously recall all the facts about their reading. Imagery questions requiring the child to give answers which do not have any textual support are optional. It is not clear how these questions might add to understanding the reader's processing of print. As evaluations of comprehension, both the Oral and Silent Reading Tests are generally inadequate.

The Listening Comprehension Test contains brief paragraphs used to determine comprehension. However, no allowance is made for listening skill and experience as prerequisites to understanding. Here again, the tests are heavily weighted with questions requiring factual recall. The value of this test and how it could be used by classroom teachers are open to question.

The oral reading, silent reading, listening comprehension, and supplementary paragraphs contain other weaknesses. No information is given for how reading levels were assigned to the paragraphs. The first paragraph in each test appears to be at the primer level. However, comparability of the paragraphs is questionable. Sentence length, syntactic complexity, and vocabulary vary. In most paragraphs there is at least one sentence which is significantly longer than the others in the paragraphs. Careful examination of the content of the paragraphs reveals such inconsistencies. For example, according to the Fry formula, oral reading paragraph number seven is estimated to be at the ninth grade level.

The paragraphs are very short and therefore provide limited content on which to evaluate comprehension. They are also straightforward, factual "reports." Lack of interest in several of the paragraphs could seriously affect the child's score. The selections focus on traditionally male interests, e.g., building, basketball, baseball, railroads, etc. All but four references to people and animals are male. Although several boys and men are described as productive and competent characters, no girls or women are. Three female references are to: 1) Muff, the kitten, 2) the mother hen, and 3) a cat. The only paragraph mentioning a girl is entitled. "The Little Girl" and describes a little girl searching for her mother in a train station. She sits and waits while a *man* tries to fix her mother's car. Her mother arrives and takes her home. Both the mother and the girl are portrayed as passive. The following statement appears in the silent reading paragraph about basketball: "Opinion differs as to whether it is a satisfactory game for girls." The sexism reflected in the test reveals its age.

Decoding/Encoding Sections

The Word Recognition and Word Analysis Test consists of four graded lists of individual words. They are presented to the child by flashing one word at a time on a tachistoscope, a manila holder with a slot through which a word is flashed for approximately one-half second. The test has some value as an assessment of the store of words the student knows instantly by sight. Since there is no contextual aid, the examinee must rely heavily upon visual information. But the sight vocabulary assessment value of this test is offset to a considerable degree by the limited number of words available for use with each of the two levels. Diagnosis of difficulty is made by noting the errors made on flash reading and then again on a second chance "analysis" of the words missed. The child's score in the word analysis part of the test depends upon the number of words sounded out after not being immediately recognized. The child could, therefore, achieve a very low score on the analysis section even though he or she had a high score on the word recognition simply because there was a limited corpus of words available to analyze. The words are quite varied to test different word attack skills.

There are three subtests on letter recognition: 1) Naming Letters, in which the child names rows of upper and lower case letters; 2) Identifying Letters Named, in which the examiner names letters and the child identifies them, and 3) Matching Letters, in which the child is shown a letter at a time for two to three seconds on the tachistoscope and then matches it with letters listed in the Record Booklet. A fourth optional test, Writing Letters, is offered. Several suggestions for administering this test are made. The relation between results obtained here and on other parts of the test is not explained.

Visual Memory of Words—Primary is a tachistoscope test in which a word is flashed and the child then identifies it and marks it on the list of words given in the Record Booklet. Visual Memory of Words—Intermediate is the same test with a more difficult word list. The primary list contains nineteen words and the intermediate contains fifteen. The intermediate list includes words which are probably not in the speaking or reading vocabulary of the average intermediate-grade student. Several words on the primary list may be in the vocabulary of those students. There are also several foils which might only confuse the children. The content validity of these tests is therefore questionable.

There are three tests of the auditory analysis of word elements. Hearing Sounds in Words—Primary tests the child's ability to separate initial and final sounds in spoken words. The examiner dictates the words one at a time. The child in turn must identify the word in which the initial or final sound matches that of the dictated word. The words from which the child must choose the matching sound are difficult; therefore, it is presumed that the skill being tested is the recognition of letters corresponding to isolated sounds. Learning to Hear Sounds in Words is a test for those students who cannot do the primary test. The examiner sounds out the names of the letters *m, s,* and *f,* one at a time, and pronounces words in which the sounds appear in the initial position. The child must repeat the sound. After the child appears to know all three sounds, the examiner dictates other words and asks the child to point to the letter that corresponds to the initial sound in that word. The purpose of the test is "to discover the severity of difficulty in perception of sounds in words." It appears that severe difficulties in the perception of sounds in words may be revealed by this test. However, readers who don't know these three particular initial sounds might have great difficulty learning three sounds at the same time in one short session. The implications of the results of this test for teaching are again unclear. The Sounds of Letters test requires the child to give the sounds represented by lower case letters of the alphabet and sixteen phonograms. Suggestions for teaching strategies again are described.

The purpose of the Learning Rate Test is "to discover the degree of difficulty the child has in remembering words taught." It is to be given to the nonreader or the preprimer reader. The test provides for brief exposure of a word on a tachistoscope and discussion of its meaning. After being exposed to and discussing several words, the child is asked to identify them on a list. Context is considered briefly in this test; however, considering recent research in comprehension regarding the importance of contextual clues, the validity of this test in measuring learning rate in reading is questionable, since the child is asked to identify words in isolation.

The final three subtests are the Phonic Spelling of Words Test, the Spelling Test, and the Handwriting Test. The purpose of the Phonic Spelling Test is "to discover the child's ability to spell words as they sound." Since the word list contains infrequently used words, the test appears to measure that ability. The purpose of the Spelling Test is not defined;

presumably, it attempts to diagnose spelling difficulties, since a checklist of difficulties is given. The Handwriting Test is to be analyzed according to another checklist. As in the subtests of reading, the various checklists are useful to the experienced teacher. No rationale is offered for the inclusion of the various subtests. If one accepts the premises that these skills can be isolated and that they are the skills to be developed in a reading program, the purpose of most of the subtests can be inferred. However, the purposes of the Spelling and Handwriting Tests are completely unclear.

The Individual Record Booklet helps the examiner to summarize the results of the Analysis. The Checklist of Instructional Needs provides a good overview of the child's difficulties. The Record Booklet also includes an outline for other data which might be significant in developing an individualized reading program. However, the Profile Chart which appears on the cover of the Individual Record Booklet and which provides a grid for plotting the data from the Analysis should *not be used under any circumstances* because standardization deficiencies prevent reliable comparison of the subtests.

Conclusions

The strength of the Analysis lies in the various checklists of difficulties. However, one must have considerable background in reading to make effective use of these checklists. The Manual of Directions states that the test should be given by experienced teachers and that "Its administration is best learned under the direction of a person who has had experience in the analysis and correction of reading difficulty." No guidance is offered as to how to interpret difficulties noted and their interrelationships. The difficulties are focused on specific skills. Therefore, the Analysis may encourage the teaching of isolated decoding and encoding skills with little concern for the development of comprehension.

In selecting a test or using scores from this test, teachers should be cognizant of the deficiencies in norming, reliability, and validity of this test. As the publisher cautions, the Analysis should be used for recording observations of the difficulties as outlined and should be considered only one diagnostic tool in developing reading programs, and certainly a limited one at best.

Gates-McKillop Reading Diagnostic Tests

Edition   Second
Authors   Arthur I. Gates and Anne S. McKillop
Publisher Teachers College Press
Copyright 1962
Reviewer   Sherry Gable, University of Northern Iowa
Critiquer Carol Santa, Kalispell, Montana, Public Schools

Overview

The Gates-McKillop Reading Diagnostic Tests is a 1962 revision of the Gates Reading Diagnostic Tests originally published in 1926. It is a standardized, individually-administered, diagnostic test battery presumably appropriate for grades 2 through 6, although no such specific grade designations are indicated in the test material itself. This diagnostic instrument "aims at discovering causes of reading deficiency, in terms of students' unique handicaps. It seeks answers to the question: "What particular skills are undeveloped and which ones are matured to a 'normal' or superior degree?" There are eight subtest sections with as many as 28 test scores (if all are administered) to accomplish this aim. The complete focus of the test is on word recognition and word attack skills, no provision being made for assessing reading comprehension. The authors suggest that a comprehensive evaluation should include consideration of any reading achievement tests administered within the past six months.

Available test materials include the Test Materials Booklets, Forms 1 and 2, the Pupil Record Booklet, Forms 1 and 2, a Manual of Directions, and a tachistoscope. The test is basically a power test rather than a speed test. No overall time limits are given for any subtests and administration time is variable. Approximate administration time for the entire test battery is 60 minutes. Time may vary depending on the number and nature of the tests selected for the student.

The various components of the test battery are:

    I. Oral Reading (7 paragraphs)
    II. Words: Flash Presentation (40 words)
    III. Words: Untimed Presentation (80 words)
    IV. Phrases: Flash Presentation (26 2-4 word phrases)
    V. Knowledge of Word Parts
        1. Recognition and Blending Common Word Parts (23 words)
        2. Giving Letter Sounds (26 letters)
        3. Naming Capital Letters (26 letters)
        4. Naming Lower-Case letters (26 letters)
    VI. Recognizing the Visual Form of Sounds
        1. Nonsense Words (20 words)
        2. Initial Letters (19 words)
        3. Final Letters (14 words)
        4. Vowels (10 words)
    VII. Auditory Blending (15 words)
    VIII. Supplementary Tests
        1. Spelling (40 words)
        2. Oral Vocabulary (30 words)
        3. Syllabication (20 words)
        4. Auditory Discrimination (14 words)

Description and Evaluation of Subtests

One group of subtests (I-V plus Syllabication VIII-3) measures decoding, i.e., production skills, while another group of subtests (VI-VIII) measures encoding, i.e., recognition skills. For diagnostic purposes, the tests measuring decoding abilities of the student are more closely related to the actual reading process, providing more direct types of information for determining reading deficiencies, and are a more valid measure of actual reading capabilities.

The manual states that "not all children will need to be given all the diagnostic tests." A student's performance on the initial test of a section is used to determine whether further testing is required on that section. The authors strongly suggest that the examiner be sufficiently well informed about the skills necessary for learning to read so that only the essential tests needed are selected for obtaining diagnostic information.

It is not necessary to give the tests in any particular order. The organization of the test booklet is such that the more comprehensive tests are presented before the more specific tests. There are two prevailing philosophies regarding order of presentation. Giving the more comprehensive tests first is more effective. If the more complex tests are passed, then the skills required for the less complex tests are presumed mastered. If the more comprehensive tests are failed, then the easier, more isolated ones are given. A second diagnostic approach, however, is that the student should be given the easier tests first so that he will experience success before failure. The examiner needs to make this decision based upon knowledge of the particular child being tested.

The Oral Reading subtest is presented as a continuous narration divided into seven separate sections. The first four are arranged into separate sentences, the final three in paragraphs. The last paragraph is reminiscent of archaic dialogue ("maybe we shall permit thee") and seems inappropriate for the target age-group. This subtest is in dire need of revision. The content and vocabulary are very outmoded. It would be helpful to apply a readability formula to the paragraphs in order to determine the difficulty level of the various sections. There is no measure of understanding whatsoever; this important reading aspect will need to be assessed with other instruments. The manual suggests that a silent reading achievement test be used to get a measure of comprehension and that, on the average, the oral reading score will be the same. This is not necessarily true and not a useful comparison. Reading authorities have consistently alluded to the fact that silent reading achievement tests tend to overestimate the reader's comprehension performance and do not provide avenues for assessing comprehension problems. Reading errors from the first four paragraphs are analyzed in terms of omissions, additions, repetitions, and mispronunciations. No consideration is made for self-corrections. Further analysis of the mispronunciations is made in terms of reversals; initial, medial, or final errors; or wrong word parts. The number of errors is translated from a raw score to a grade equivalent score which is then compared with the student's actual grade position and rated as Very Low, Low, or Normal.

In order to have a valid measure of the student's oral reading ability, the diagnostician needs to possess certain competencies such as: 1) the knowledge of and ability to use a marking code or system; 2) the ability to record word pronunciations phonetically; 3) the ability to record errors accurately and systematically; and 4) the ability to classify errors correctly.

The Words and Phrases subtests, both flashed with a tachistoscope, determine the student's ability to recognize words instantly. The subtest called Words: Flash provides the examiner an opportunity to observe the methods a student uses to attack unknown words presented in isolation. This subtest can be very frustrating for the poor reader. The manual directs the diagnostician to have the child read all forty words. Word difficulty quickly progresses from easy words (how) to words very difficult in pronunciation and meaning (lamentation). Moreover, the word list contains very few easy words. For the preprimer to first grade reader, this test usually provides little diagnostic information.

A very helpful device in the Pupil Record Booklet is a checklist of difficulties in oral reading and word pronunciation. Difficulties which may be identified include such problems as reading word by word, inadequate phrasing, rapid reading, etc. In order to make maximum use of this checklist, the examiner needs to focus on observing the student's other essential reading behaviors. The next group of subtests measures, in decreasing complexity, word attack abilities such as pronouncing and blending nonsense words (usually of one syllable), giving single letter sounds in isolation, and naming lower and upper case letters. It would seem consistent with the organization of the test that the Syllabication test be the first in this section since finding, combining, and blending multisyllabic words is more integrative and complex than recognizing and blending basically one syllable words. The raw scores on these five subtests are directly converted to ratings of Normal, Low, or Very Low in comparison to the student's oral reading grade equivalent score.

Subtests VI (Recognizing the Visual Form of Sounds) to VIII (Supplementary Tests), excluding the Auditory Blending,

Individual Tests

Syllabication, and Auditory Discrimination tests, are designed to measure encoding skills. Words or letters are presented and the student is asked to identify the correct word or letter contained in the word pronounced by the examiner. The Letters and Vowel portions present only single letter sounds and only one example is provided for each sound. This would seem to be an adequate number of items for each measured behavior for an analysis of errors. Tests such as these where the child is asked to produce the phoneme equivalent of single consonants are of very questionable value. In some cases fairly accurate phoneme representations can be produced (/n/, /s/, /m/) but in other situations a single phoneme cannot be isolated from subsequent vowel representations (/g/, /y/, /p/). The diagnostician should be aware of this problem when making decisions about using the subtest. Probably the best solution, next to not giving the test at all, would be to present the child with just the letters having single phoneme representations. Also, children not exposed to synthetic phonics instruction may do very poorly on this test even though they may very well have the concepts of letter sounds within word contexts. The diagostician should know the instructional history of the student.

The Auditory Blending subtest requires the student to blend a word pronounced by the examiner such as "s-im-ply" into "simply." Subtests VIII-4, Auditory Discrimination, might be the final test in the series since the ability to distinguish whether two pronounced words are the same or different usually precedes the ability to blend words. But it has no norms and cannot be interpreted within this framework.

Spelling and Oral Vocabulary are two of the supplementary tests. The words for the spelling test are taken from the untimed words section. Following this test is a checklist. The Oral Vocabulary subtest asks the student to select from among four reading choices the correct definition of a word given by the examiner.

Technical Aspects

No description is given of the norm group. It would be helpful to have a description of the norm group in terms of size, grade level, sex, IQ, time of testing, socioeconomic status, and other pertinent variables. As no such data exists, test users will be unable to determine to what extent their students correspond with the standardization group. Thus, it is nearly meaningless for a test user to interpret his or her students' results with the norms provided. A second problem is that only one set of norms is provided for both forms for each subtest. The publisher claims that the forms are of equivalent difficulty, but no evidence of equivalence is given.

However, the most serious criticism concerns the lack of data on reliability or validity. Reliability indices should be computed by the alternate-form and test-retest procedure for each subtest so that the user can judge the accuracy of a score on one form of the test in comparison to the score on the other form of the test.

Another type of reliability information specific to the test which should be provided is the standard error of measurement for both raw score and grade equivalents for each subtest on both forms so that some estimate could be made concerning the variability of the student's "true" score.

No type of validity is reported. While the tests do appear to have validity for use as a screening measure for assessing students' word attack abilities, users of the test still need to survey the content of the test to determine if the tests are an appropriate evaluative instrument for their particular curricular objectives. As the tests are purported to be an armamentarium of diagnostic devices, some data should be provided which demonstrate the independence of the subtests. Subtest intercorrelations are lacking but there is no evidence regarding the degree of overlap between subtests.

Conclusions

The strengths of the Gates-McKillop Reading Diagnostic Tests include the Manual of Directions which is well-organized and clearly written. A special plus is the provision of information given in the section for scoring and interpretation of the test scores and the section which suggests other subtest performance comparisons.

The basic weaknesses lie with some technical aspects and with the lack of any provision for assessing comprehension, the incomplete norm data, and the absence of validity and reliability data.

Some suggestions for using this test battery follow:
1. Use it as an informal assessment tool, ignoring norms.
2. Study the response patterns for possible remediation but be aware of the small number of subtest items.
3. Use it in conjunction with other types of evaluative instruments for more comprehensive assessment.

This test, like all diagnostic tests, provides performance measures; examiners or teachers diagnose.

Gilmore Oral Reading Test

Edition   Second
Authors   John V. Gilmore and Eunice C. Gilmore
Publisher   Harcourt Brace Jovanovich
Copyright 1968
Reviewer   Randall Ryder, University of Wisconsin at
             Milwaukee
Critiquer   Sean Walmsley, State University of New York at
             Albany

Overview

The Gilmore Oral Reading Test consists of two parallel test forms (C and D) which, according to its authors, provide teachers with a means of analyzing the oral reading performance of students in grades one through eight. Each form of the test consists of ten graded passages which in their entirety are a continuous story. Gradation of the difficulty of each passage was controlled by constructing passages according to 1) number of words in the passage, 2) the average grade level placement of words according A Core Vocabulary (Educational Development Laboratories), 3) number of polysyllabic words in passage, 4) mean number of words per sentence, and 5) number of complex sentences in passage. A summary of each of these aspects is provided in the examiner's manual. Five literal recall questions accompany each passage and are administered orally by the examiner.

Passages are individually administered to the subjects from a hardbound spiral booklet containing both forms of the test. The examiner's copy of the test consists of a softbound student record blank which contains the same paragraphs as the spiral test booklet; the five literal comprehension questions;

a space to note the time (in seconds) for oral reading; and a chart for tallying errors of substitution, mispronunciation, insertion, hesitation, repetition, omission, words pronounced by the examiner, and disregard of punctuation. While the time for testing varies across subjects, approximately 15-20 minutes are required for test administration.

The directions for test administration are detailed and clearly written. Because the test requires the examiner to time each reading with a stopwatch and record oral reading errors while the subject is reading, substantial training and practice is required for accurate scoring.

Norms

Percentile ranges, a performance rating (poor, below average, average, above average, superior), grade equivalent scores, and stanines are provided for the accuracy and comprehension scores while only performance ratings are provided for the rate score. These norms are based on the testing in 1967 of 4,455 students in grades one through eight located in six school systems geographically distributed throughout the country. While the normative population was purported to have included a variety of socioeconomic backgrounds, no attempt is made by the authors to define their proportional representation. Both local norms and norms for various socioeconomic groups in interpreting test results are lacking. Users should consider developing norms which reflect their particular student population.

Reliability

The reliabilities reported for the two test forms are alternate-form correlation coefficients for each of the three test scores. These coefficients are based on relatively small and inadequately defined samples of students in third and sixth grade who were administered each form of the test within two-week intervals. The test manual reports correlation coefficients on the accuracy score of .94 for third graders and .84 for sixth graders. Coefficients for the comprehension score were .60 and .53 for third and sixth graders respectively. And coefficients for the rate score were .70 for third graders and .54 for sixth graders. It is apparent that the correlation coefficients for the comprehension and rate scores fall below generally accepted standards for reliability. Of equal concern is the failure of the authors to provide information about the stability of test scores across examiners. This information would be useful, given the somewhat subjective nature of scoring this test.

Validity

One of the greatest weaknesses of the Gilmore test from a technical standpoint is the absence of evidence regarding the concurrent and content validity of the revised test forms. Instead, the authors refer to the validation studies of the original forms of the test which were conducted on an extremely small and undefined sample of students. Even on the original validation studies, no attempt was made to correlate comprehension, accuracy, and rate subscores despite the authors' claim that the test analyzes oral reading performance.

While the manual fails to provide evidence of the test's content validity, inspection of the passages reveals two elements which would appear to lessen content validity. First, the passages themselves display content similar to that found in the basal readers of the 1950s. Consequently, subjects' interest and attention to the passage may be somewhat limited. Second, the inclusion of literal recall comprehension questions alone may not accurately reflect the comprehension found in the students' reading instruction. Therefore, it is suggested that users evaluate the content of the passages and criteria for obtaining the three test scores in light of the content and objectives of their reading programs.

An assumption of the test is that "if one can read well orally one can read well silently." Although this is generally true, there are two serious problems with this assumption. One, the Gilmore test provides no evidence that it does correlate well with silent reading. Two, even though such a correlation may generally exist, an oral reading score may not necessarily accurately reflect the silent reading level of the reader. A correlation, no matter how large, does not necessarily indicate equivalency between the two variables. Therefore, as the name of this test indicates, it is a measure of oral reading.

Evaluation of the Test

Test administration and scoring are done simultaneously. Subjects are instructed to begin reading the passage which is two grade levels below their grade placement, e.g., a sixth grader begins reading the fourth grade passage. If the subject makes more than two oral reading errors on that passage, he or she is presented the next lower passage(s) until two or fewer errors are attained (basal level). The examiner then continues to present the passages in their increasing level of difficulty until the subject makes ten or more oral reading errors (ceiling level). The criteria for recording errors are as follows:

1. Substitution—a real word substituted for the word appearing in the passage.
2. Mispronunciations—a nonsense word voiced as a result of false accentuation, mispronunciation of vowels or consonants, omissions and/or insertions, or addition of one or more letters.
3. Word Pronounced by Examiner—a word which is not pronounced by subject after 15 seconds is voiced by the examiner.
4. Disregard of Punctuation—failure to note any punctuation.
5. Insertion—a word inserted in the text of the passage.
6. Hesitation—a pause of 2 seconds prior to the pronunciation of a word.
7. Repetition—a word, part of a word, or group of words repeated.
8. Omission—one or more words omitted.

Literal comprehension questions are posed by the examiner following the examinee's completion of each passage. Separate computations are made for each of the three test scores. The accuracy score is computed by the rather complicated procedure of subtracting the number of errors on each passage from ten, then summing this score across all passages read, then adding points by extrapolation, for each paragraph below the student's basal level. The comprehension score is computed by totaling the number of questions answered correctly on each passage and extrapolating points on passages which fall above the student's ceiling level and below the student's basal level. Finally the rate score is obtained by calculating rate in seconds by summing the total number of words read in each passage, then dividing that quantity by the total number of seconds for all passages read.

According to the authors, the criteria for determining what constitutes an oral reading error were determined from "a study of error frequency based on data obtained from an initial administration of the test, and an analysis of published oral tests." It is apparent that the criteria for errors accurately reflects the prevailing views on oral reading diagnosis during the 1950s and early 1960s. However, in light of recent views regarding the nature of oral reading errors, these criteria may not be consistent with those currently practiced by diagnosticians and teachers. Most noticeable is the test's criterion for scoring mispronunciations. For example, according to the authors, pronouncing the word *ground* as "grounds" and pronouncing it as "wheelbarrel" would be errors of equal magnitude. Users concerned with obtaining additional diagnostic information on the nature of mispronunciations may wish to develop a separate checklist to analyze these errors as to their semantic, syntactic, and/or graphophonemic aspects.

Summary

The Gilmore Oral Reading Test consists of graded passages individually administered to subjects. The test yields three scores: accuracy, comprehension, and rate. Although careful detail was taken in the construction of the passages, their content is dated; hence, the passages are likely to be uninteresting to many students. The use of the tests for diagnostic evaluation must be viewed with caution in light of inadequate reliability data and the absence of information about the test's validity. Probably it will measure adequately the accuracy of oral reading of meaningful material—if that is the examiner's intent. The validity of other uses is unknown.

Individual Tests

Peabody Individual Achievement Test

Authors   Lloyd M. Dunn and Frederick Markwardt
Publisher   American Guidance Service
Copyright 1970
Reviewer   Karen Hansen, Normandale Community College
Critiquer   Joe Peterson, Sterling, Illinois, Public Schools

Overview

The PIAT Manual says the purpose of this test is "to provide a wide-range screening measure of achievement in the areas of mathematics, reading, spelling, and general information." In addition, the Manual cautions, "It is not intended as a diagnostic instrument in a particular subject matter area.... Further, it is not intended as a precise measure of the exact level of an individual's achievement."

The total test battery consists of Mathematics, Reading Recognition, Reading Comprehension, Spelling, and General Information. It is designed for individual administration for grades K-12, testing time being 30 to 40 minutes. Each of the five subtests has 84 items except Reading Comprehension which has 66, beginning with item 19. Only the reading subtests are reviewed here.

Each of the subtests is introduced by a Demonstration and Training Exercise. Not all items within a subtest are given to each student; instead, a "basal level" is determined from a suggested starting point and a "ceiling" established when errors are made in five of seven items. The "ceiling" score minus the errors determines the raw score for that particular subtest. Raw scores may be converted into grade level equivalents, percentile ranks, and/or standard scores. The variety of measures in addition to the inclusion of an IQ scale (if such a measure is available) provides a number of possible profiles for interpretive purposes.

Even though directions for administration are clear and complete, extensive familiarization is required on the part of the examiner, particularly in terms of presentation format, scoring, pronunciation of the spelling test, and decisions about starting and ending points within subtests. For persons unfamiliar with individualized testing, training is essential.

Reading Recognition Subtest

The initial 18 items require naming of letters. Sounds of letters are not included here but do comprise items 11-14 of the Spelling subtest. Items 19-84 consist of pronouncing single words. This is justified in the manual because it is time-efficient and easy to score accurately. But the validity of this subtest, whether it reflects what readers do in the reading process, is never mentioned. Instead, it is stated that "skill in reading aloud correctly can be an important ability and is often considered a mark of a cultured person." Educators should be aware that the authors of the PIAT are not certain what, other than word pronunciation, this subtest measures nor how scores on it should be interpreted (what instructional strategies to employ if an examinee scores low on it).

Educators should be aware of three other aspects of this subtest's validity. One is that items were included "not...because they tested a critical content area...but to provide a wide-range, quick screening test." Thus, the authors determined this subtest's validity, in part, by item discrimination and difficulty. This doesn't make the test invalid but neither does it really clarify what it measures.

Two, the examiner must make judgments about the correctness of pronunciation. While pronunciations are subject to regional and dialectical differences, the authors are adamant that only a standard dictionary pronunciation is acceptable. In fact, a training tape is available, which has been "found helpful in training...testers," which gives the "creditable pronunciations for each of the 66 words."

Three, the authors acknowledge that this test's scores may be confounded by "acculturation factors" that change "the meaning of attack skills." They warn users to be aware of this when interpreting low scores much above the fourth grade level where a subject may have very sophisticated word attack skills but be unable to pronounce a word acceptably because it is not in his hearing or speaking vocabulary. They also caution examiners to interpret scores obtained by subjects in the first grades in light of the subjects' type of reading instruction. Requiring word pronunciation to be exact but urging examiners to take instructional method and cultural sophistication into consideration would seem to make any accurate interpretation of this score very difficult and unlikely.

Reading Comprehension Subtest

This subtest consists of single sentences to be read silently only once followed by the presentation of four line drawings, one of which best illustrates the sentence. A very narrow definition of reading comprehension has been used, understanding of a single sentence at the literal level only. This should have the advantage of producing a homogeneous test. On the other hand, it may not adequately reflect the range of tasks readers are expected to perform in actual reading situations. In other words, the validity of the test would be questioned by most educators. Furthermore, to provide differentiation at the upper level, sentences of such complexity are required that contrived and artificial sentences are resorted to, e.g., "In their secluded bivouac in an inaccessible sector of the realm a horde of guerillas grovelled before a mysterious deity."

Last, errors in interpreting the artist's representation may not be errors in reading comprehension.

For these reasons, it is questionable whether this subtest really measures what most educators define as reading comprehension.

Standardization

Following field testing, the test was standardized on 2,889 cases, slightly over 200 at each grade level 1-12 and 159 in kindergarten, in 27 communities in 9 regions throughout the United States. Great care seems to have been taken to select a sample representative of children in the mainstream of urban, suburban, and rural public school education, according to 1967 census data.

Peabody Individual Achievement Test

In each geographical division, groups of trained supervisors trained and supervised the examiners who actually administered the tests.

Although questions could be raised about some points of standardization, this test seems as well standardized as all but the very best individualized tests.

Reliability

Reliability data are based on a one-month testing interval at 6 different grade levels. Reading Recognition reliability coefficients are in the high 80s, with the exception of grade 3 which is .94. These are adequate. But Reading Comprehension reliabilities have a median of .64, while never exceeding .78 (grade 1). These are reasonably low. Such low correlations produce fairly large standard errors of measurement which means that the scores lack precision and dependability.

Conclusions

The cautions in the manual, combined with a careful consideration of the validity and reliability of these subtests, should be of concern to educators attempting to make any decision about reading achievement on the basis of this test. Despite impressive standardization procedures, these subtests can't be recommended very highly. These scores should be taken with the proverbial grain of salt and, if something other than an initial gross screening is desired, other more valid and dependable measures should be used.

Individual Tests

Sucher-Allred Reading Placement Inventory

Authors   Floyd Sucher and Ruel A. Allred
Publisher Economy Company
Copyright 1973
Reviewers Catherine W. Hatcher, University of Northern
Iowa
Katherine Treadway, Kansas State University

Overview

The Sucher-Allred Reading Placement Inventory (RPI) is to help a teacher place a student appropriately for reading instruction and is composed of two parts, a Word Recognition Test and an Oral Reading Test. The specific information that may be gained includes:

1. A student's independent, instructional, and frustration reading levels.
2. Common word recognition and comprehension errors made from oral reading.

Word Recognition Test

The Word Recognition Test contains twelve word lists, ranging in difficulty from the primer level through the ninth grade reading level. The words on each list were taken from the graded reading paragraphs. The primer and first grade lists contain fifteen words each and the other lists contain twenty words each. The authors suggest that the Word Recognition Test has three purposes:

1. To find an approximate instructional reading level.
2. To identify a probable starting level for the Oral Reading Test.
3. To determine achievement in word recognition.

The vocabularies from several basal readers (the manual did not specify which) were surveyed to determine the words most frequently used and the grade placement for each. Excluding proper nouns, words were randomly selected for each grade level. The authors stated only that "a study was conducted to determine which words were the best predictors for each grade level" (p. 6). The population data analysis and specific results of this study were not stated.

The administration and scoring procedures are clearly explained in the manual. The directions state that the teacher is to begin this test at a level at which the student is likely to make no errors. The student should continue to read from succeeding levels until five or more words are unknown at one level. It is suggested that the level at which five or more errors (or miscues) occur should be near the student's instructional reading level.

Oral Reading Test

The Oral Reading Test contains twelve reading paragraphs graded in difficulty from primer level to ninth grade reading level. The authors state four purposes for this test:

1. To evaluate word recognition skills.
2. To determine comprehension strengths and weaknesses.
3. To identify the student's reading level.
4. To enable the teacher and student to become better acquainted.

The administration procedures are clearly stated, including a marking code for word recognition errors. Examples of each type are given along with the coding symbol.

A sentence to be used by the teacher for motivating the child is given. The child reads orally and the teacher records the errors made during reading. The booklet is then removed and the child is questioned about the selection. Five types of questions are used: main idea, facts, sequence, inference, and critical thinking. To aid the administrator in scoring, sample responses are given for the questions. Errors in word recognition are summarized by type and counted along with the number of comprehension errors. The paragraph is judged to be at the independent, instructional, or frustration reading level according to a table of errors for both word recognition and comprehension.

When the pupil has completed the Oral Reading Test, the teacher is instructed to tally the total number of countable word recognition errors and comprehension errors to complete the summary section of the student test booklet. Specific and general teacher observations are encouraged on the form as well.

Comments

The interpretation of the error patterns from oral reading is mainly quantitative and is apparently based on the premise that an error is "the problem." Recent reading research based on psycholinguistic principles indicates that more complete diagnostic information would be yielded from a qualitative as well as a quantitative analysis of errors. In addition, many educators question how much useful information can be gained from analyzing frustration level reading errors. While the teacher is cautioned in the manual to take into account the errors made at different levels, the diagnostic teaching information gained from the analysis would probably be increased significantly by excluding those errors from frustration level reading.

Two problems are apparent in the format of the Oral Reading Test. First, because only one form is available, teachers may feel that a child's reading performance should be evaluated by considering only oral reading. Second, limiting the number of each type of question asked per paragraph results in an inadequate number of items per category. For example, if a pupil reads three paragraphs, he or she may answer only three factual questions during the entire test. This is unrealistic from the standpoint of typical instructional procedures and insufficient for diagnostic comparison of categories.

Both interest and readability were employed as criteria for the selections of the Oral Reading Test. While the method of assessing interest is not stated, the passages appear appropriate in content for the intended grade level. Readability was calculated on selections A-F by the Spache Formula and on selections G-L by the Dale-Chall Formula.

Content validity for the RPI was established through vocabulary control and readability (Spache and Dale-Chall results are reported in the manual). However, no data are provided about the predictive validity of the test nor about the accuracy of the word recognition and comprehension criteria.

Since there is only one form and because there is no evidence that the test was either tried out or normed in any way, there is no way of judging the test's reliability.

Conclusions

The RPI includes some features that make it attractive and practical for the classroom teacher to use. The manual is designed to provide a good, clear explanation of the concepts required for *tentatively* placing students in appropriate reading materials as well as of the specific procedures to be followed in using the RPI to increase the accuracy of placement. The procedures for gross screening include using a wide variety of reading material and ways to use the material. The teacher is encouraged to develop and use his or her observation skills.

A Class Record Form is also available to help the teacher organize and manage the needs of the students within the class. Many teachers need help in organizing the data collected on the pupils for effective reading instruction.

Generally, the Sucher-Allred Reading Placement Inventory appears to be a useful tool for the classroom teacher *in combination with other procedures* for gathering data on the reading performance of students. However, since there are no reliability data provided, two cautions must be exercised. One, results should be viewed as estimates to be confirmed or rejected by additional information; and two, the results should not be used to measure reading achievement but rather only as guidelines in placing children in reading material.

Woodcock Reading Mastery Tests

Author   Richard W. Woodcock
Publisher American Guidance Service
Copyright 1973
Reviewer Martha Rapp Haggard, University of California at Berkeley
Critiquer Nancy Smith, Kansas State University

Overview

The Woodcock Reading Mastery Tests (WRMT) are a battery of individually administered reading tests, which were designed for use in grades K-12, but which appear to be most usable in grades K-6. They are intended to be particularly useful for clinical or research purposes. The two forms of the tests, A and B, are packaged in ringbinder easel kits which contain all of the test materials, the examiner's manual, and response forms. The tests use basal and ceiling criteria to determine which items are to be administered to each individual. Response forms are designed for hand scoring, with additional scoring services available from the publisher.

Five tests are included in the battery: Letter Identification, Word Identification, Word Attack, Word Comprehension, and Passage Comprehension. Letter Identification is made up of 45 items which require naming of letters presented in eight typefaces (4 manuscript; 2 cursive; 2 "specialty"). Word Identification consists of 150 words ranging in difficulty from basic sight words to words difficult for superior students in the twelfth grade. Word Attack consists of 50 nonsense word items beginning with one-syllable CVC combinations and progressing to multisyllabic words. The Word Comprehension test is composed of 70 analogy items. The student is required to supply the last word in a four-word sequence, e.g., "boy-girl: man-_____." The final test, Passage Comprehension, is a modified cloze format with 85 items. Each item requires that the subject read silently a phrase or a one-to-two sentence passage and supply an appropriate response for one missing word. Each test yields a separate score; in addition, an "Index of Total Reading" score is derived from the combined test scores.

Administration and scoring procedures are fully described in Part II of the manual. Along with the basic instructions, the manual provides a discussion of the principles of good test administration which is both comprehensive and detailed. Supplementary directions and alternative administration procedures are also included for each test. Administration time for the entire battery is listed as approximately 30 minutes; however, this reviewer has found that for many students, especially disabled readers, total administration time is closer to 50 minutes.

A variety of scores can be derived from the raw score, some usual ones (percentile rank) but others unique to this test. Grade equivalent scores are interpreted differently from other standardized tests. For any one subtest, three grades scores, E, R, and F, can be obtained, each indicating a different level of competency. The R level represents "the predicted performance of a subject on tasks accomplished with 90 percent mastery by average students of the referenced grade level; E, 96 percent; F, 75 percent." These grade scores, called Relative Mastery scores, need to be thoroughly understood by users of the results so as not to be confused with the more commonly used definition of grade scores. The part of the manual describing these unusual scores lacks clarity and needs to be studied rather than just read.

All of these scores, and others, are reported in the nine separate tables located in the back of the examiner's manual. Because of the number and variety of scores provided, these tables may appear hopelessly confusing to some using the test for the first time. Careful reading of Part III of the manual, however, will clarify their use. Directions are clear, precise, and detailed.

Test Development and Standardization

The procedures used in developing and standardizing the WRMT were exceptionally thorough. A large number of test items were collected, then some of the less valuable were eliminated. A total of 36,000 calibration tests were individually administered to children in grades K-12. An uncommon statistical procedure, Rasch-Wright, was used to determine which items "fit the model." Acceptable items were assigned difficulty values to produce the Mastery Score Scale upon which the unique grade scores mentioned above are based. From the pool of acceptable items, Forms A and B were compiled and normed on a stratified random of 5,252 students in 50 school districts. Communities chosen as part of the sample were distributed according to geographic location and six socioeconomic variables. Complete explanation of norming procedures and the data obtained are provided in the examiner's manual. The technical quality of the tests is most impressive.

The most troubling and disappointing aspect of the tests' construction is the absence of any explanation as to why these particular subtests were decided upon and why some unusual formats, e.g., analogy in Word Comprehension, were used. The statement that opinions of professionals in the field of reading "were most helpful in determining which tests would have the greatest merit for clinical and research purposes" is unenlightening. The validity of the subtests is therefore quite uncertain, as is pointed out below.

Reliability

Split-half reliability and test-retest alternative-form reliability were determined from tests administered to approximately 100 second grade and 100 seventh grade students during the spring following the original norming study. The manual states that the same students were used for both reliability studies; however, no other description of the sample is given. Although the AGS catalog states that split-half reliabilities were calculated for grades 1, 2, 4, 7, and 10, the data for grades 1, 4, and 10 were gathered from "Pre-A" tests that were not identical to either of the final forms. Those results are therefore irrelevant to a discussion of final form reliability.

Split-half reliabilities for the individual tests generally fall within an acceptable .90 to .99 range. The major exception is Letter Identification, which yielded .79 and .86 for Forms A and B, respectively, at the second grade level, and .02 and .20 at the seventh grade level. The only other low reliabilities reported were .86 and .83 for seventh grade Word Comprehension.

Test-retest alternate-form reliabilities were calculated on the basis of a one-week interval between administration of Forms A and B. Approximately half of the students at each grade level were administered Form A first and then Form B. The other half took the tests in reverse sequence. For the second grade sample, alternate form reliabilities range from .84 (Letter Identification) to .97 (Total Reading). At the seventh grade level, however, only one test, Word Identification, reaches an acceptable level of .93. The two lowest are Letter Identification (.16) and Word Comprehension (.68), with the remaining tests falling in the .78 to .85 range.

Based upon both the split-half and alternate-form reliabilities, it appears that some care must be exercised when interpreting scores, especially for older students. Given the level of reliability obtained, Word Comprehension scores might best be viewed as tentative until confirmed; furthermore, the usefulness of the entire battery as a before and after measure of reading achievement for secondary students seems severely limited.

Validity

Two major sources of evidence for the validity of the WRMT are outlined in the examiner's manual; however, neither appears adequate. For content validity, the reader is referred to Part I of the manual, where the objectives and descriptions of the tests are given, and a statement that the items represent "actual tasks drawn from the domain of reading in that there are tasks of identification, tasks of word attack, and tasks of comprehension." No effort is made to compare these tasks to similarly identified tasks found in instructional materials or on other tests.

Comparative data were used in the Multimethod-Multitrait Matrix procedure; however, the "methods" compared were Form A and Form B of the test. Since this procedure assumes that two *independent* methods of measuring the same trait are to be compared, the results are questionable at best; they appear to be little more than additional reliability data.

Users are therefore left on their own to determine the validity of these tests.

Evaluation

The major weakness of the Woodcock Reading Mastery Tests appears to be that in attempting to serve all, they serve few well. Although they were designed for use in grades K-12, their usefulness above grade six is highly suspect. The Letter Identification subtest is designed specifically for assessment of a skill associated with beginning reading and is, in fact, optional for use with older readers. The use of unusual letter shapes and typefaces may make this test of little interest to most reading practitioners. Some caution is advised when using this test with adolescents; experience indicates that they consider it an unimportant and demeaning task. Word Identification is also only partially useful in grades 9-12. Disabled readers above 10th grade often "top out," i.e., do not miss five consecutive items, on this test, thus indicating that there are not enough items of sufficient difficulty to assess performance adequately. In such instances, while analysis of oral reading errors is still possible, grade equivalent and percentile scores must be interpreted with care.

The formats of the Word Attack, Word Comprehension, and Passage Comprehension tests cause additional concern. The use of nonsense words to assess word attack skills is considered by many to be a questionable practice, and can only tangentially qualify as "task drawn from the domain of reading." Students who have been taught with a program that gives heavy emphasis to word attack skills may score well on this test while students who have not, may do poorly in relation to other tests. Results must therefore be viewed in light of instructional approaches, particularly with primary age students.

The analogy format of the Word Comprehension test presents even more serious problems. First, and most important, is the concern that such items measure something besides word knowledge, and that there is no way to tell when they are measuring what. Analogy items are a recognized measure of abstract reasoning, classifying abilities, etc., and are a part of numerous intelligence and general aptitude tests. Second, contrary to the author's claims, solving analogies is *not* a common school (or reading) task. Student responses indicate that students must learn the task *as they are being tested*; the four practice items are not sufficient. This is supported by the fact that, in this reviewer's experience, students rarely achieved basal level performance at the estimated reading level starting point, even when that same point was adequate for all other tests. Furthermore, it has often been observed that students consistently missed one type of analogy at levels where other types were answered with ease. All of these factors lead to the conclusion that the Word Comprehension test does not measure a clearly defined word comprehension skill; results may be contaminated to an unknown degree by variations in such abilities as abstract reasoning, general intelligence, and learning speed.

The modified cloze format of Passage Comprehension is based on the assumption that understanding, or comprehension, of a passage may be inferred by the correct replacement of a missing critical word; it is therefore an indirect measure of comprehension which, depending on one's view of the reading process, may or may not be as valid as the more traditional direct-question approach. The WRMT allows for individual differences by accepting synonym replacement; however, interpretation of scores is cast into doubt by the absence of any means to determine how students arrive at their answers. Examiners are prohibited from probing responses, with the result that scores may be artificially inflated or deflated by factors unrelated to passage understanding. One suspects, however, that the test errs more in the first sentence instance than the last; experience indicates that Passage Comprehension scores tend to overestimate achievement levels, and so must be used cautiously to place students in instructional materials.

Last, because examples of diagnostic interpretation of results are generally not presented, test users may be uncertain what to do with the results. The tests seem best suited as a global screening measure, particularly for identifying children experiencing difficulty in learning to read. The user must collect additional data from other sources before developing diagnostic prescriptions.

In general, the Woodcock Reading Mastery Tests, though flawed, are a usable instrument for assessing some aspects of reading performance at the elementary school level. Test users however must understand the tests' weaknesses and interpret scores accordingly.

Group Tests

Individualized Criterion-Referenced Tests

Edition   Second
Author   Unlisted
Publisher   Educational Development Corporation
Copyright   1976
Reviewer   Anthony Petrosky, University of Pittsburgh
Critiquer   Lillian Putnam, Kean College of New Jersey

Overview

The eight levels of the Individualized Criterion-Referenced Tests (ICRT) are sequenced by instructional objectives arranged from the least to the most difficult. The tests roughly correspond to the eight elementary grades. Each test booklet assesses eight objectives via sixteen questions with two test items per objective. Each test kit contains tests for the designated level and two levels below, a teacher's manual, scoring templates, and an orientation cassette. One complete testing of a mastery level requires five test booklets (including 40 objectives, 80 items). The tests are not timed and can be administered individually or in small groups. Although the length of the tests varies, administration time is estimated at thirty to forty-five minutes. Levels 1-3 of the test booklets are consummable.

The test manual says that "students are tested at the levels at which they are working. In a third grade classroom for example, some students may be tested on objectives at level two, a number at level three, some at level four, and a few at levels five and six. Thus, the students in a given grade or classroom may be taking a variety of tests at a variety of levels." In this way, the testmakers claim their instruments assess specific knowledge and skills that students have learned and determine knowledge and skills appropriate for students' next instructional steps.

Objectives

The ICRT's 304 objectives range from phonic identification as a paper-and-pencil task to literal and inferential comprehension, literature, and content field reading. The Reading Objective booklet lists objectives by sequence at each level with traditional reading skills phrased as behavioral objectives indicating what the student will do. At the early elementary levels, they represent operations such as letter-sound correspondences, word recognition (in and out of context), consonant classifications, vowel identifications, and, at later grades, operations such as putting sentences in proper sequence, and identifying main ideas, grammatical features, author's purpose, genre, etc. The content areas are represented with items using material from social sciences, mathematics, laboratory experiments, newspapers, literary selections, and analogies. The literary type objectives include such operations as identifying mood, character, foreshadowing, etc.

While the coding of objectives to various instructional material is helpful and practical for teachers, some of the objectives such as paraphrasing or finding "another way to say exactly 12 feet" are open to criticism for assessing skills other than reading. A number of the items at the early grade levels focus on skills such as spelling and word endings that are certainly language arts objectives but questionable as reading objectives. Likewise, the inclusion of verbal mathematical items is questionable.

While the objectives appear specific, comprehensive, and well sequenced, the test manual does not give theoretical, empirical, or practical rationales for the selection of the objectives, their sequencing, or their classification according to levels of difficulty. Without information like this, potential users have no clear way of gauging the appropriateness of the tests. Although statistical procedures were used to calculate relative degrees of difficulty among the tests and to scale and rank each objective, the manual doesn't explain the procedure in any helpful way. Consequently, the issues of objective goodness and appropriateness—the powers underlying criterion-referenced tests—are left open to criticism. This lack of rationale linking items to objectives raises serious questions about the quality of the test's construction, the degree to which the objectives are validly measured by the items, and the degree of assurance that test users can feel about the results.

There is another, more technical, problem with the ICRT. When testmakers work from lists of objectives, the definitions of how items are to test a specific objective may be unstated or ambiguous. Consequently, the item pool—those items available for testing a specific objective—may be composed of varied item types. When this is the case, it is misleading to say that any one item represents the others, or that all items are equally representative of ways to assess the specific objective. Without item representativeness, scores can only be interpreted in terms of the specific individual items. Thus, we don't really know whether both items are indeed assessing the same objective. An explanation of rationale or explicit statistical procedures could have mitigated this problem. Neither of these is provided.

To further complicate matters, the power of criterion-referenced tests rests upon the number of items used to test a specific objective—the more items (up to a point), the better. Including only two items per objective on the ICRT is insufficient for reliable measurement.

Passages

The passages used to assess comprehension range from pictures and single words at the elementary levels to complex sentences and rather lengthy prose selections at the higher grade levels. Generally, the passages are related to grade level by length—the passages get longer as the levels increase in difficulty. Content area passages are included and passage types reflect both expository and literary prose. The verbal mathematical items are interesting for their inherent requirement that students understand the problem through reading and then solve them arithmetically. Although these verbal mathematical items have suffered a lack of popularity over the past twenty years, they are quite well constructed in the ICRT; however, they are still open to criticism as assessing mathematical thinking more than reading.

The comprehension passages may have a sex bias. In Booklet No. 257, for example, of the eleven paragraphs, six have male characters, one has a female character, and four have no sex reference.

Since passage selection is not discussed in the manual, important issues such as passage difficulty, bias, length, and representativeness are passed over. In the light of the powerful role played by passages in reading tests, the omission of selection specifications for determining the acceptability of passages is a serious problem. Potential users need to know, for example, whether the comprehension passages tap various kinds of reading materials, e.g., newspapers, magazines, stories, etc., and whether the selections are timely, sufficiently lengthy for readers to form a mind set, and free of bias. It is also crucial for users to know how passages were determined as being suitable for specific levels and ages. None of this information is available for the ICRT.

Items

The test manual claims that each item is a four-choice question but the sample test packet includes consistent use of two- and three-choice items in addition to items whose stems are not complete but rather left blank for the insertion of the correct response. A number of the four-choice items are presented with foils listed vertically while others are presented with them listed horizontally. Even though the directions are clear, the switching of foil formats could pose problems for unsuspecting, hurried, or careless students. Furthermore, the use of the terms "long and short vowels" in some of the early elementary material is questionable, as many instructional materials use "glided and unglided" instead.

Test Specifications

The ICRT was field tested on 80,000 children from 1972-1973 and then again in a final version in 1973-1974 on a nationwide sample of 400,000 students. The manual states that "decision rules in classifying student score patterns for the ICRT have a high degree of reliability and validity in describing student performance with respect to objectives." Nevertheless, the specifications do not address the issues of how objectives were chosen and sequenced (except to say they were sequenced statistically), how and why passages were chosen, what makes passages appropriate for any given level or age, or how an item assesses an objective.

According to the specifications, the ICRT was correlated with a norm-referenced test with correlations ranging from .71 to .86. Even though correlations of this size would usually be considered adequate for most tests, the manual doesn't indicate the usefulness of this comparison since norm- and criterion-referenced tests usually provide quite different kinds of information. Neither is the norm-referenced test named.

Results

An impressive feature of the ICRT is the computer printout giving detailed objective-by-objective results for a group and/or individual. These results not only evaluate the student's performance but also direct the user to specific pages that can be found in available material for this instruction. These computer printouts may lend a false air of sophistication to the test. One problem is the use of only two items to measure each objective, a procedure that doesn't adequately provide for guessing by individuals (although it is more trustworthy for group data). Another is that we have no assurance, except the publisher's word, that items are in fact measuring the same objective. The first is a matter of reliability, the second of validity. Thus these computerized results, seemingly so scientific and objective, need to be interpreted very cautiously.

Conclusions

If a teacher or a school system decided to use part or all of the ICRT, a significant amount of work would be necessary to isolate objectives relevant to the curriculum and an equal amount of work to determine whether the selected items assess the objectives they claim to. Determining whether the items measure what they claim to can be handled in a number of ways. The most reliable checks on item validity require field tests, then statistical evaluations, or formal consensus from experts working with the technical specifications. Teachers, on the other hand, can check for face or content validity simply by deciding whether the items do what they claim. However, this check on validity is weaker, more time consuming, and difficult.

Generally, the lack of explicit theoretical, empirical, or practical rationales is a serious problem with the ICRT. Equally troubling is the omission of careful attention to passage selection. The item constructions pose problems serious enough to present difficulties for students taking the test and, thus, to warrant criticism. Hopefully, future editions of the ICRT will be more carefully developed than was this one.

Prescriptive Reading Inventory Levels A and B

Authors   CBT/McGraw-Hill Staff
Publisher CBT/McGraw-Hill
Copyright 1972
Reviewer   Edward L. Robbins, Indiana University
Critiquer William E. Blanton, Appalachian State University

Overview

The Prescriptive Reading Inventory (PRI) is a criterion-referenced test of specific reading skills. It is organized into six overlapping levels designed to test preprimary through sixth grade reading skills. Levels A through D cover the grade levels 1.5-2.5, 2.0-3.5, 3.0-4.5, and 4.0-6.5 respectively. Levels I and II are designed to cover reading skills below the 1.5 grade level. Because of space limitations in this monograph, this review will cover only Levels A and B.

Level A, the "Red Book," assesses performance on 34 reading skills determined by the test developers to be the most common and appropriate reading skills for grade levels 1.5 through 2.5. Level B, the "Green Book," covers 41 skills considered to be most appropriate for the 2.0 through 3.5 grade levels. The skills included in both levels are oganized under the following reading skill areas:

1. Recognition of Sound and Symbol
2. Phonic Analysis
3. Structural Analysis
4. Translation
5. Literal Comprehension
6. Interpretive Comprehension
7. Critical Comprehension

The approximate time required to administer either of the levels is three hours. It is suggested that the administration of the test be divided into sessions not more than 45 minutes each. Both levels are designed to be machine scored by the publisher.

The test results are reported in an individual profile format which shows, by skills, those that have been mastered, those needing review, and those not mastered. Also available for each student is a set of alternatives among specific locations in the student's basal program where the teacher can find ideas and activities for instruction and practice in the unmastered skills.

Each skill in Levels A and B is tested with three or four multiple-choice items, presented in clusters, which makes it possible for a testing session to be ended after any cluster.

Consideration in Selecting a Criterion-Referenced Test

The most important consideration in selecting a criterion-referenced reading test is the correspondence between the skills covered by the test and those of the reading program. In order to best determine the extent of this match, the skills of the test must be stated in terms which specify not only the reading behaviors, but also the criteria for meeting them. The PRI unequivocally specifies both the reading behaviors and the conditions under which they will be displayed.

In deciding whether the match between the PRI objectives and the objectives of the reading program is close enough to justify the use of the PRI, it is necessary to consider a variety of factors.

1. Many of the word recognition objectives in the PRI are tested by items that assess the skill in an activity that involves the total reading act. While it is desirable to be able to perform a skill in the context of meaningful reading activities, testing of skills in such a context often complicates the analysis of reading performance. A specific skill may be completed with a variety of strategies—it is not always possible to infer, for example, that a student who selects a word from a set of words, only one of which has the correct initial consonant to complete a sentence with a word omitted, can recognize initial consonant sounds. Performance might be attributable to sight word recognition or

the use of context rather than the ability to recognize initial consonant sounds.

2. The context in which any PRI skill is tested should be checked to determine that the testing context is consistent with the context of instruction. If the instructional program teaches a skill in a particular way, it is important that performance of the skill be measured in a similar manner.

3. The distribution of PRI skills across the various reading areas should approximately match the distribution of skills in the school's reading program. The scope and sequence of reading programs vary. Some programs place heavy emphasis on phonics or other decoding skills from the beginning, while others emphasize comprehension. Of the 34 skills in Level A, 15 fall into word recognition categories, while 12 are comprehension and 7 are vocabulary and context meaning skills. A similar pattern is followed in Level B. The PRI appears most appropriate for those reading programs that lay equal emphasis on the various skills of reading. It should be noted, however, that Levels A and B do not measure study skills.

4. The placement of skills in the various levels of the PRI should correspond reasonably well with that in the school's reading program. A criterion-referenced test is generally administered to make an instructional decision. A student who has mastered a skill should be excluded from instruction or provided with enrichment activities. Students who have not mastered a skill or who need practice should receive additional instruction. Consequently, the measurement of skills should be placed immediately before or after instruction. This does not mean, however, that it is inappropriate to measure performance at some time after instruction, particularly if the purpose is to determine whether mastery has been retained.

A final descriptive feature of the PRI which should be considered is the performance criteria used in determining whether a child has mastered an item, needs review of it, or has failed to master it. The technical report provided by the publisher suggests that criteria for the different performance levels were based on factors such as the performance in the test tryouts of students who had been taught the skills prior to testing compared with that of those who had not and the sensitivity of a skill to instruction (the extent to which students who could not perform a skill prior to instruction were able to perform it after instruction). While the use of the procedures to establish cutting scores on criterion-referenced tests is an accepted practice, the technical report provides no specific data on the use of these procedures in determining criterion scores on the PRI. As it turns out, all skills measured with the same number of items have the same performance criteria. Even with the limited number of items provided to measure the PRI skills, it seems unlikely that the evidence that was supposedly used would result in the same criteria for all objectives. The scores required to meet PRI performance categories are as follows:

Number of Items	Mastery Score(s)	Review Score(s)	Nonmastery Score(s)
3	3-2	1	0
4	4-3	2	1-0
5	5-4	3-2	1-0
6	6-4	3-2	1-0

Validity

The skills included in the PRI were identified through a comprehensive analysis of the skills covered by five of the most widely used reading series in the United States. This analysis, which included a page by page review of the series and an identification of the objectives that were either explicitly or implicitly covered, resulted in 1,245 objectives, which were then categorized. The objectives were further reduced to include only those that covered skills directly related to the reading process and that were included in most or all of the series examined. This careful and comprehensive approach to selecting the final set of objectives to be included in the PRI tryout tests seems more than adequate to insure the content validity of the tests.

Construct validity for the PRI was assessed through a variety of procedures including typical item analysis and item difficulty procedures, as well as the comparison of performance on selected PRI objectives with performance on the reading subtests of the California Achievement Test—70. While the construct validity evidence obtained through these procedures is varied, it tends to support the content validity evidence that the PRI tests what it purports to test. However, it must be noted that test validity requires test reliability, and the lack of specific objective-by-objective reliability scores for the PRI must be considered in determining its total validity.

Readability

Technical data provided by the publisher of the PRI indicate that the reading levels of the vocabulary and reading passages used in the PRI test items were controlled where possible by using vocabulary considered to be at least one grade level below the PRI level in which it was used and by using language structure that was no more complex than that found in the typical reading program at levels corresponding to the PRI levels. While both of these considerations are important first steps in controlling readability, no rationale is given for the lack of information on the computed readability levels resulting from these efforts. Potential users of the PRI must examine the reading levels of the PRI carefully to insure that they are appropriate for the intended students.

Reliability

In analyzing the reliability of a criterion-referenced test, it is important to understand that tests such as the PRI that evaluate multiple skills are not single tests, but batteries of tests. The set of items designed to assess each of the PRI skills constitutes a separate test. Accordingly, reliablility on a skill-by-skill basis is needed. No such reliability data are provided for the PRI.

Although the PRI test development staff indicates that such reliability information could have been provided, they chose instead to use what they term an unorthodox approach to reliability. They selected a small sample of objectives from each level—seven from Level A and eight from Level B—and constructed special tests of ten items each paralleling the items of the PRI and used these special tests as the basis for their reliability study. The special tests were administered to students who had taken the PRI, and the two performances were correlated. Also, Kuder-Richardson Formula 20 reliability coefficients were computed for the special tests. No information is provided on how to interpret the significance of the reliability scores, which ranged from .67 to .88 for the special tests, or the correlations between the two tests, which ranged from .42 to .75. One might interpret this data as meaning that the reliability of the special tests ranged from moderate to high. On the other hand, the correlations between the PRI test and special tests ranged from low to moderate. A correlation of .42 suggests that part of the PRI does not measure what the special tests measure or that part of the PRI has low to moderate reliability. Test developers argue that there are more acceptable ways to establish the reliability of criterion-referenced tests. Potential PRI users should want to know what the reliability of the PRI tests are.

The position of the PRI test developers in defending their unorthodox approach to reliability is equally dismaying. The PRI staff, while admitting that measuring a skill with a small number of items produces a reliability score that is less than ideal, defend their decision to provide a small number of items for each test by concluding that "more information is obtained about a student's specific strengths and weaknesses in reading by measuring a large number of fairly specific objectives with a few items than by measuring a few general objectives with a large number of items." Most authorities would agree with this statement if they had confidence that the information obtained by testing many objectives with a few items was accurate. However, few would agree if the reliability of such tests was so low as to provide results that were of questionable reliability.

Conclusions

Levels A and B of the PRI are machine scored, criterion-referenced tests designed to measure the most common reading skills found in grades 1.5 through 3.5 of the reading program. However, in order to be both manageable and efficient, a test of specific reading skills must be limited, both in terms of the number of objectives covered and the number of items used to test each objective. The implication is that prospective users of the PRI must carefully compare the objectives covered by the PRI with the objectives covered by their own reading program. The implications for the limited number of items per test is the lack of test reliability and the potential for errors in the test results of the PRI.

However, for school systems desiring a test that can be used to assess a fairly large number of reading skills and that requires relatively little time to administer but that may provide results subject to some inaccuracies, the PRI would appear to be an appropriate instrument. Because it is particularly important to have the results of instructional tests as soon after testing as possible, the time required for the publisher to return the results should also be an important consideration to potential test users.

Stanford Diagnostic Reading Test

Authors   Bjorn Karlsen, Richard Madden, and Eric Gardner
Publisher Harcourt Brace Jovanovich
Copyright 1976
Reviewer Leo M. Schell, Kansas State University
Critiquer Josephine S. Goldsmith, Rutgers University

Overview

The Stanford Diagnostic Reading Test (SDRT) is a lengthy, technically sophisticated standardized group test, which measures several major components of the reading process and which is designed to give particularly accurate data on low achievers. It comprises four levels, Red, Green, Brown, and Blue, which together cover the end of grade 1 up through grade 12 and community colleges, with two parallel forms at each level. Because of space limitations in this monograph, only the Red Level for the end of grade 1 and for grade 2, and the Green Level for grades 3 and 4 are reviewed here.

The SDRT is based on a concept of reading as a developmental process with four major components: decoding, vocabulary, comprehension, and rate. As reading achievement grows, the relative importance of each of these components alters, and these changes are reflected in the slightly different subtests at each level and the way in which the same skill is measured at different test levels. This concept seems conventional and generally uncontroversial. However, numerous reading theorists are beginning to question such a hierarchical model.

Subtests for the Red and Green levels are:

Red Level (Grade 2)	Green Level (Grades 3 and 4)
Auditory Vocabulary	Auditory Vocabulary
Auditory Discrimination	Auditory Discrimination
Phonetic Analysis	Phonetic Analysis
Word Reading	Structural Analysis
Reading Comprehension	Reading Comprehension

Decoding Subtests

The stated purpose of the Auditory Vocabulary subtest is to provide information about pupils' language competence, or knowledge of common meanings of words frequently found in primary grade reading materials, without requiring the pupils to read. The subtest is entirely dictated to the students by their teacher. The teacher says, "Rings and necklaces are kinds of dishes, furniture, jewelry" and the pupils mark a drawing in the test booklet. The manual states that rigid criteria, including frequency of use for pupils in grades 1-3, were established for selecting words. However, after consulting the Harris-Jacobson Basic Elementary Reading Vocabulary and the American Heritage Word Frequency Book, the present reviewers concluded that at least 15 percent of the words do not meet these criteria and are inappropriate for the test level. Included are such infrequently used upper grade words as *garments, odor, employee, conflict, ornament* and *neglect*. And the Red Level contained more infrequently used, higher-level words than did the Green Level. It is difficult to understand how such words were included in a test designed primarily for low achievers. But the intended use of the test's results is equally puzzling. The manual's suggestion that pupils scoring low on this subtest should receive some vocabulary instruction before much progress in reading comprehension can be expected may, in light of the above criticisms, simply be wrong. The reviewers believe the results are potentially useful as indicators of reading potential, but research is needed to substantiate this speculation.

The Auditory Discrimination subtest requires pupils to determine whether the same sound occurs at the beginning or the end of two dictated words (Red and Green Levels) or in the middle of them (Green only). No reading is required.

Part B of this test at the Green Level is unique. Pupils are to decide in what part, beginning, middle, or end, two pronounced words sound alike (e.g., *touch* and *come*). The experience of these reviewers suggests that neither instructional material nor teachers usually present auditory discrimination tasks without specifying what part of the words should be compared. Thus this test may involve more complex analytic tasks and a heavier memory load than the auditory discrimination tasks faced in common reading instruction. It is probably not simply an auditory discrimination test, and teachers should definitely supplement its results with additional information on the auditory discrimination performance of their pupils.

The Phonetic Analysis subtest is a more complicated task than the two subtests discussed above. At the Red Level, the teacher pronounces the name of an object pictured on the test form, and the pupils select the initial, medial, or final letter or group of letters of the word. It requires, in part, more than simple phoneme-grapheme association. For example, for "clip," pupils must choose from *ap, op, ip,* and *up.* At the Green Level, pupils must independently read a stimulus word with one or more underlined letters and then read three response words and choose the one containing the sound represented by the underlined letter (s) in the stimulus word. Clearly this is a formidable task, as shown by the fact that there is greater spread between the mean and the top score on this subtest than on any other subtest. Also, the test may measure significantly more than its title implies. Being able to read all the words in an item may be a more significant factor than knowing sound-letter relationships. Giving phonics instruction to pupils scoring below average on this subtest may be unnecessary and unwise.

The Structural Analysis subtest (Green Level) has two parts, A and B. Part A requires pupils to identify the first syllable of selected two-syllable words. A stimulus word is given, followed by 3 choices, e.g., invent - i, in, inve, all of which the pupil reads independently. Part A presents 3 syllables, two of which can be put together to form a real word. Part A requires pupils to find visually (or to remember) syllables, while Part B requires them to blend syllables together. Even though no other test that we know of uses the technique used in Part B, and even though we have never seen a teacher or commercial instructional material employ it, it seems enough related to the task pupils must perform with unrecognized polysyllabic words to be considered valid, particularly if teachers will use other information to confirm or refute this subtest's score.

The Word Reading subtest (Red Level) presents a drawing followed by three lines of three words each, all of which pupils read independently. One word in each line is associated with the drawing, e.g., cake, party, fun. Only words found in reading material for grades 1, 2, and 3 are said to be used, and a check of Basic Elementary Reading Vocabularies confirmed this. The subtest requires children to do some logical reasoning as well as pronounce the words correctly. This task seems closely enough related to what pupils must do in much beginning reading instruction for it to be considered valid.

Comprehension Subtest

The comprehension subtests at both levels use relatively traditional and accepted measurement procedures suitable for the level of reading development of the pupils for whom the tests were intended. Also, the correlations between the SDRT and the Stanford Reading Tests are high enough, .90 or above, to remove any doubts about the test's concurrent validity.

On the other hand, by providing separate scores for literal and inferential comprehension, the Green Level perpetuates a myth that most measurement and reading experts have been trying for years to destroy. Without being specially constructed, no test has ever been able to establish the existence of discrete comprehension skills that can be interpreted separately. Drahozal and Hanna (1978) showed that, in a silent reading test similar to the SDRT, it was impossible to distinguish among groups of items categorized as measuring three different comprehension tasks; they seemed to be measuring the same thing. Moreover, the authors and publishers of the SDRT have omitted any theoretical rationale or empirical data which might support such a distinction in this test. Teachers should ignore the Literal and Inferential scores and use only the Total Comprehension score.

Test Development and Standardization

The procedures followed in constructing and standardizing the SDRT were thorough and professional.

After the content was identified, objectives formulated, and items written, the items were tried out in representative school systems. The results were scrutinized and forms of the test were assembled from usable items.

These forms were then standardized in school districts chosen to parallel the 1970 U.S. census with regard to geographic area, urbanization, system size, ethnic group, and socioeconomic status. The number of pupils tested seems to have been adequate although exact numbers are not stated. Also, the Reading Test of the 1973 Stanford Achievement Test was administered to pupils in the standardization sample so that the results of the two tests would be compared to give some idea of the validity of the SDRT. In general, the scores of the test should be as accurate and reliable as was the standardization.

The validity of the test rests primarily upon the instructional objectives identified as a result of the analysis of curriculum guides and major reading series that was done prior to item writing. The test, therefore, is generally valid for schools using such materials. However, individual schools, particularly those using "nontraditional" techniques such as the language experience approach, may find it less appropriate. Minor validity problems with subtests are mentioned under the discussion of each one.

The SDRT deserves high marks in several areas. The subtests have an adequate number of items to produce a highly reliable test. Care has been taken to include ethnic minorities in the norming group, and sex stereotyping in content has been avoided.

Two aspects of the test that are acknowledged in the manual but not stated as emphatically as we think they deserve to be are the following:

1. Distribution of scores. Scores intentionally do *not* have normal distributions; on most subtests, above average scores are bunched together. Sometimes only 4-6 raw score points separate the highest possible score from the mean while several times this skewedness is so severe that the ninth

stanine (the highest possible) is even omitted in the norm tables. Therefore, it is probably a waste of time to give this test to pupils performing decidedly above grade level in reading.

2. Progress indicators. For several subtests, the authors have established arbitrary cutoff scores of between 50 and 75 percent. Pupils achieving below this specified raw score on a subtest are said not to have sufficient competence in this skill. But no specific justification is given as to the why these particular points were established. Instead, it is implied that test users are to trust the authors' decision. Equally questionable is the dichotomous nature of this score. If Alicia gets 18 items right on a subtest while Ivan gets 17, Alica is said to have demonstrated sufficient competence and receives a plus, while Ivan has insufficient competence and receives a minus. Because of this dichotomy, statistical data in the manual indicate that, particularly for the Red Level, there is a fairly large margin of error. Progress indicators should not be the sole information used in making diagnoses.

Conclusions and Recommendations

1. This is probably the best constructed group diagnostic test available.
2. This test is not a complete assessment of reading achievement. For example, it does not indicate a child's instructional reading level—the level at which a child should be placed for formal, systematic instruction. It does not measure how well pupils use syntactic and semantic cues in their reading or their knowledge of sight words. This means that other ways of testing and gathering information about these unmeasured areas must be used for a total reading profile of examinees.
3. The instructional grouping recommendations in the manual should be used very cautiously. Test results are global rather than detailed and are inadequate for individual instructional prescriptions, e.g., two pupils with identical scores on Phonetic Analysis may have vastly different instructional needs. Additional diagnosis is necessary to determine which specific subskills are lacking.
4. Because of its complexity and the time required to administer it (over two hours), it should *not* be given unless a

well-devised plan has been formulated for using the results in an instructional program.

5. It should be given only to selected pupils. Giving it to pupils definitely achieving above grade level would probably be a waste of time and give misleading results as well.

6. Because there are some validity and reliability problems with some subtests, it is imperative that test scores be combined with other information before definite instructional decisions are made. Using only scores from the SDRT subtests may lead to some inaccurate and unwise decisions.

Reference

Drahozal, Edward C., Hanna, Gerald S. Reading comprehension subscores: Pretty bottles for ordinary wine. *Journal of Reading, 21* (February 1978), 416-420.